BRETON

Nadja

D1392481

Roger Cardinal

Reader in Comparative Literary Studies
University of Kent at Canterbury

Grant & Cutler Ltd
1986

Library of Congress Cataloging-in-Publication Data

Cardinal, Roger.
  Breton, Nadja.

  (Critical guides to French texts: 60)
  Bibliography: p.
  1. Breton, André, 1896-1966. Nadja. 2. Surrealism (Literature) I. Title.
II. Series.
  PQ2603.R35N333 1986   843'.912   86-25667
  ISBN 0-7293-0255-5 (pbk.)

I.S.B.N. 84-599-1730-4

DEPÓSITO LEGAL: 2.047 - 1986

Printed in Spain by
Artes Gráficas Soler, S.A., Valencia
for
GRANT & CUTLER LTD
55-57, GREAT MARLBOROUGH STREET, LONDON W1V 2AY
and
27, SOUTH MAIN STREET, WOLFEBORO, NH 03894-2069, USA

Contents

References

References to the text and illustrations of *Nadja* are to the 1972
Folio edition (item *8* in the Bibliography) and take the form of
the page number in parentheses. An oblique stroke, rather than
a hyphen, between page numbers indicates that the text is inter-
rupted by an illustration. References to other works comprise an
italicized number relating to the entry in the Bibliography, plus
page numbers, thus: *16*, pp.58-59.

1. Introduction

What kind of a book is *Nadja*? In an account of a dream, André Breton once described himself looking through his bookshelves and finding a multi-volumed work he did not recognize. Haphazardly plucking out one of the volumes, he found it to be some sort of philosophical treatise, except that on the title page, instead of a standard heading such as *Logique* or *Morale*, there figured the startling rubric *Enigmatique* (*14*, p.41).

If we were to imagine a shelf of books devoted to the ideas and attitudes encompassed by French Surrealism, then *Nadja* might well be that volume we pick out by chance and find to be an exercise in 'Enigmatics' — a curious discipline which seeks to come to terms with phenomena which resist ultimate clarification. Dense and idiosyncratic, *Nadja* has exercised a steady fascination over its many readers since its publication in 1928. Its reputation as a classic text of early Surrealism rests on the fact that it exemplifies a number of central tenets of the movement; its power to fascinate has to do with the disturbing ways in which this is done.

Evolving out of the interaction of a group of talented young poets who had met up in Paris towards the end of the First World War, Surrealism as a collective enterprise had by 1928 settled into a relatively coherent shape. The publication of Breton's *Manifeste du surréalisme* in 1924 had given the movement its charter and identified its cause — namely, the defence of the rights of the imagination in an era of depressing intellectual and social conformity. Emerging as it did at a point of maximum impetus in the public history of the movement, *Nadja* is in one sense the natural fruit of collective experiment and interaction, and as such may be said to typify the spirit of early Surrealism. Equally it remains a private statement marked by its author's most personal impulses and inhibitions, and as such tends to come across to the uninitiated as tantalizingly obscure.

One basic reason for this effect of obscurity is easily given: *Nadja* tends rather to state than to explain. In documenting surrealist experience, it concentrates on *what* happened at the expense of *how* or *why* something happened. The episodes presented in the book carried Breton to an existential and intellectual breakthrough in grasping the import of a surrealist approach to existence. Yet their emotional aftermath was so great that he was unable to communicate what he had learned in any clearcut way. Indeed, at the time of writing, Breton seems to have positively shied away from any sort of confident comment or theory as being in some way inimical to a proper appreciation of surrealist experience. The point needs to be firmly stressed, since it is, in my view, wrong to suppose that *Nadja* at all addresses itself to orthodox modes of understanding. Such an elusive and eccentric text can only be taken on its own slippery terms. In the *Manifeste*, Breton had given notice that 'le langage de la révélation se parle certains mots très haut, certains mots très bas, de plusieurs côtés à la fois. Il faut se résigner à l'apprendre par bribes' (*16*, p.142).

Rather than a book *about* Surrealism, *Nadja* is essentially a demonstration *of* Surrealism. As such it is a fragile and mysterious entity, as valuable yet as fleeting as the perception of surreality itself. In this study, my aim has been to honour the idiosyncrasies and protean appearance of a work which defies the straitjacket of any single critical perspective. Admittedly I have sought to structure my observations, to make explicit some of Breton's more obvious hints (often by drawing on concepts spelled out in subsequent works like *Les Vases communicants* or *L'Amour fou*), to discuss as lucidly as I can certain matters concerning the darker side of mental life — in short, to draw conscious intellectual propositions out of the author's veiled intimations. Further, I have not hesitated to invoke material extraneous to the text wherever this sheds light on its meaning. More than most books, *Nadja* is an intertextual phenomenon, being intimately bound to other writings by Breton, not to mention those of his fellow surrealists. (It is, for instance, ideologically inseparable from Louis Aragon's *Le Paysan de Paris*, which came out only two years earlier, though space prevents my pursuing the numerous analogies between these two classics.) Again, the avowedly 'documentary' cast of the work makes it impossible to isolate it from the extra-literary contexts of Breton's private life, his position within the surrealist group, the history of Surrealism at large, and indeed contemporary cultural and political events. The student of *Nadja* may wish to bring into play biographical, historical and even topographical information: a street-plan of Paris, for instance, is an almost indispensable accompaniment to the text. He may need to exercise himself as detective, sociologist, psychologist or psychoanalyst, as well as literary critic. The great wealth of discussion on *Nadja* (see Bibliography, section IV) testifies to the capacity of this text to renew itself across time and to remain perhaps the happiest of hunting-grounds for commentators on Surrealism. At certain moments, I have been nagged by a sense of critical impropriety, as when I refer to Breton's mistress by her real name, rather than the anonymous cipher 'X' which he uses in the text. But does not the author himself insist that authentic writing must address the authentic details of people's lives (see p.18)? And is it not better to maximize one's knowledge of what lies beyond the periphery of the text, the more fully to alert oneself to resonances within it? Breton himself seems to have ratified such a multi-perspectival approach when he once wrote: 'Et d'ailleurs la signification propre d'une œuvre n'est-elle pas, non celle qu'on croit lui donner, mais celle qu'elle est susceptible de prendre par rapport à ce qui l'entoure?' (*17*, p.15).

I am aware that this study is not entirely a work of literary criticism in the strict sense. But then, *Nadja* is not a work of literature 'in the strict sense', but a text arising out of a crisis concerning the function of literature, one which adopts a militant stance with regard to the conventions and limitations of the literary mode in the interests of communicating a new, enhanced perspective on the function of books within people's lives. As should be axiomatic with any text of a poetic kind, I have sought to avoid narrow interpretation and instead to encourage the reader to see the text as a field of multiple meanings. It seems to me that *Nadja* is best envisaged as a many-layered structure, a set of superimposed, semi-transparent patterns which, in combination, constitute the dense and poly-valent whole. I have attempted to 'peel off' some of these individual leaves and to envisage the work, by turns, as a dossier on surreality, a treatise on chance and desire, a meditation on personal identity, an enquiry into paranormal experience, a narrative of a love-affair, an oblique manifesto about a certain way of living, an anti-novel, and an exercise in the stylistics of Enigma. Doubtless there are further leaves which could be unpeeled. What I most hope is that my various readings do not come across as bald reductions of the typically hesitant nuances of the original. It is not my ambition to neutralize Enigma, but to lead the reader to the point where the impact of Enigma can be the most richly appreciated — not as puzzlement or frus-tration, but as stimulating bewilderment, the prelude to unsuspected revelation.

2. The Surrealist Dossier

A compendium of clues

Breton's book is basically the catalogue of a series of real-life incidents which struck him forcefully over a period of years. They date back at least to 1915, and culminate in the startling phenomena associated with a young woman called Nadja, with whom Breton himself had a brief affair in autumn 1926. In detailing these incidents, he tells us that, while their significance was often highly uncertain, he became progressively more convinced that he should take note of them. As an album of 'faits d'ordre inhabituel' (p.137), *Nadja* is principally offered as a *demonstration through example*, a collection of data which implicitly reflect a definition of the surrealist consciousness which appropriated them and of that elusive order of experience which we may call (despite Breton's personal reluctance to use so bold and distinct a term) surreality.

The happenings and perceptions with which we are concerned are extremely varied, and it is inevitable that we should want to sort them out. Early in the text — even before citing any instance of what he is talking about — Breton toys with the possibility of drawing up a table of categories grouped between two extremes. On the one hand there are the *faits-glissades*, highly tenuous occurrences whose impact is all but negligible. On the other, there are the *faits-précipices*, those overwhelming events which indelibly mark the surrealist's consciousness. Breton muses on several intermediate categories (pp.20-21), but later chides himself for having been tempted to formalize his data. It would, he says, be vain to expect anything from 'le trait qu'on jette en parlant en bas d'un certain nombre de propositions dont il ne saurait s'agir de faire la somme' (pp.173/175).

If one of the lessons of *Nadja* is indeed that surrealist experience cannot be appreciated in terms of quantity, but only in terms of quality, it would be futile to hope for instant illumination from a mere totting-up of Breton's examples. With this proviso in mind, I propose none the less to risk a preliminary survey of the material by grouping some typical samples under the following unpretentious headings: (a) elective places, (b) enigmatic objects, (c) perceptual correspondences, (d) recurrent motifs, (e) coincidences, and (f) encounters.

(a) *Elective places*

There are, firstly, certain locations which seem especially conducive to surrealist experiences. Of the town of Nantes, where he had spent the war-years 1915-16, Breton asserts that it is 'peut-être avec Paris la seule ville de France où j'ai l'impression que peut m'arriver quelque chose qui en vaut la peine' (p.33). The Place Dauphine in central Paris is described as a pivotal site which can hold the visitor in an insistent embrace (p.93), while the flea-market at Saint-Ouen is the perfect environment for the surrealist in search of intriguing junk (p.62). Breton speaks of certain second-rate theatres or cinemas as having qualities which belie their appearance, such as the defunct Théâtre Moderne (also evoked by Aragon in *Le Paysan de Paris*), with its blotchy mirrors, airless boxes and rat-infested stalls, and its upstairs bar like something dreamed up by Rimbaud (pp.43-44).

It is above all the city street which, in common with Aragon and other surrealists, Breton identifies as his ideal. In an earlier text he had already laid claim to it as the natural habitat of the urban surrealist: 'La rue, que je croyais capable de livrer à ma vie ses surprenants détours, la rue avec ses inquiétudes et ses regards, était mon véritable élément: j'y prenais comme nulle part ailleurs le vent de l'éventuel' (*17*, p.11). His special predilection is for the eastern section of the Boulevard Bonne-Nouvelle, where he loves to stroll in the late afternoon (p.38).

(b) *Enigmatic objects*

It is at the eastern end of this boulevard that there stands the odd seventeenth-century structure of the Porte Saint-Denis: Breton illustrates it with a photograph, commenting that the edifice is 'très belle et très inutile' (p.38). He admits to strong yet unexplained feelings about the statue of Etienne Dolet on the Place Maubert (p.26) or that of Jean-Jacques Rousseau on the Place du Panthéon (p.31). In each case, the structures seem to acquire special status to the extent that they stand out as arbitrary obtrusions within the continuum of the cityscape. They are non-functional, isolated and enigmatic, and their private meaning for Breton is quite separate from their public meaning as historical monuments.

Breton litters his text with references to smaller objects, including a piece of bronze cast in the shape of a glove (p.66), a Polynesian statuette (p.154), and an irregular half-cylinder in a casket which he purchased at the flea-market in ignorance of its function (p.61). To these may be added the books and pictures inseparable from Breton's daily life as a surrealist intellectual and collector. He speaks excitedly about picking up a mint copy of Rimbaud at the flea-market (p.63), takes the trouble to record that he bought a volume by Trotsky just moments before his fateful meeting with Nadja (p.71) — there is perhaps a hint that the acquisition precipitated the encounter in some magical way — and tells us how he has copies of his own works bound in special colours, for effect (p.84).

Pictures and drawings figure prominently in the book's visual documentation. We find reproductions of paintings by Uccello, Braque and the surrealist artists De Chirico and Ernst, as well as of the unsophisticated drawings of Nadja. On one level, the range of such images reveals Breton's aesthetic sensibility. On another, their apparent randomness of selection sets up eddies of mystery, sensitizing the reader to the presence of signs which, for the time being, point nowhere.

(c) *Perceptual correspondences*

Under this heading — which may be taken to subsume such lyrically formulated sub-groupings as Breton's 'rapprochements soudains', 'accords plaqués comme au piano', or 'certains enchaînements, certains concours de circonstances' (pp.20-21) — may be listed the instances of improbable and involuntary connexions between entirely separate facts of perception. Louis Aragon shows Breton that a hotel sign, MAISON ROUGE, can be read from another angle across the street as POLICE. The same day, Breton comes across a trick picture of a tiger which turns into an angel or a vase if tilted to either side. Breton proceeds to compound the mystery by drawing attention to the near-simultaneity of these two incidents, insisting that, although entirely irrational, 'leur rapprochement était inévitable' (p.68).

An impressive complex of correspondences arises from the words BOIS-CHARBONS, which were printed on the last page of Breton and Philippe Soupault's *Les Champs magnétiques*, the first surrealist text (see *13*, p.121). Breton narrates how, on a stroll with Soupault one Sunday, he discovered as they turned each corner that he could foretell with disturbing accuracy where these words would appear in the next street, as a notice outside the premises of fuel merchants. He stresses that he was orientated not so much by the verbal sign as by the crude picture of chopped logs that accompanies it (see illustration, p.30). This quasi-hallucinatory image seemed furthermore to be indissociable from the sound of street-music, and finally the head of the Rousseau statue. The cumulative effect of these involuntary associations was one of panic; there is even a hint of a suicidal impulse, in that Breton speaks of gazing down at the statue from his hotel window and suddenly recoiling (p.31).

(d) *Recurrent motifs*

A number of motifs recur insistently in the text, most noticeably in the section concerning Nadja herself. I will cite here those of the eye and the hand.

The eye lies at the centre of a network of imagery linked to Nadja and her meaning for Breton. The very first thing he notices about her is her emphatic eye make-up: 'Je n'avais jamais vu de tels yeux' (p.73). Breton seems to find her eyes hypnotically entrancing, as witness the one photographic 'portrait' of the woman in the form of a fourfold replication of her 'yeux de fougère' (p.129). Fervent references to female eyes — those of a fiery beauty glimpsed in Nantes, of the actress Blanche Derval, of a seductive wax figure (pp.33, 48, 179) — point to a dominant erotic fixation. That Nadja insists on drawing interlinked eyes in her picture 'La Fleur des amants' (p.139) confirms the resonances of erotic and amorous excitement.

The hand is another focal image. It appears in the form of the occult 'main de feu' which Nadja and Breton pursue through Paris (pp.116-17), as the red gauntlet in De Chirico's painting *L'Angoissant Voyage* (see p.151), or again as the ambiguous bronze glove and the sky-blue glove belonging to a woman friend of Breton's (pp.64-65). Two lines of interpretation may be mentioned here. Firstly, the hand is associated with palmistry, hence with divination, and occultism in general. Secondly, it has erotic connotations (fairly overt in the work of De Chirico) because of its implied gesture of caressing. One of Nadja's drawings depicts a glove which frames a self-portrait with heavily stressed eyes, the other features of the face being displaced by the conventional symbol of a heart within which she inscribes her own name and Breton's initials, in the time-honoured way of lovers (p.144). All these associations — of amorous union, erotic contact and divinatory insight — may be taken to be foregrounded meanings in the text, given that the eye and the hand are integral to a code of connotations exploited by most surrealist poets, Paul Eluard being the most obvious example.

(e) *Coincidences*

The narrative of the Nadja episode in particular is crammed with coincidences. Some of these are of minimal interest, as when Nadja shows Breton letters from an admirer and Breton recognizes his name as that of a misogynous judge which Eluard had wanted to cite in a recent text (pp.113-14). Others are more compelling, as when, after an evening's stroll across the city, Nadja remarks to Breton that they have wandered with no conscious intent from the Place Dauphine to a bar called Le Dauphin. Breton adds that, in one of the surrealists' games in which an animal takes the place of a person, he often finds himself cast in the role of dolphin (p.103). At another time, Nadja remarks of Breton's kiss that it is a sacred communion in which her teeth play the part of the host. The following morning, Breton receives a postcard sent from Italy by Aragon, a reproduction of part of an Uccello painting entitled *The Profanation of the Host* (p.109). The coincidence here serves to alert the reader to an underlying unease within the relationship, while serving to enhance the general sense of an irresistible spell drawing the lovers together. On another occasion, idle remarks made by Nadja as the two sit before a fountain in the Tuileries gardens chime in exactly with a passage about the rising and falling of thoughts in a book by Berkeley which Breton had just been reading. The incident is dramatized by the sequential reproduction of a photo of the actual fountain and the fountain depicted in the frontispiece of the book (see pp.99 and 101). This is one of those 'pétrifiantes coïncidences' (p.20) which point to the presence of hidden mental powers.

(f) *Encounters*

The unexpected encounter is a crucial theme within Surrealism. In *Nadja* Breton refers to many meetings with people, always with a suggestion of deeply stirred emotion. He relates his impassioned discovery of the poetry of Rimbaud in Nantes in 1915, and the affinity he immediately felt when he came across Huysmans, an author who became as intimate a friend as anyone he had met in actuality (pp.59 and 16). Real-life confrontations are detailed no less ardently. Breton tells how he first met Eluard and Péret, subsequently key figures in the surrealist group (pp.29 and 33). He recalls bumping into a girl in the rain one day who insisted on reciting a Rimbaud poem, and Fanny Beznos, another Rimbaud admirer, whom he met at the flea-market (pp.62-64). Within the pages of *Nadja* is inserted the summary of an earlier text, 'L'Esprit nouveau' (see *17*, pp.101-03), in which he tells how he and two friends encountered the same striking woman on separate occasions within the space of a few hours, each being aroused without quite knowing why (p.89).

Above all, Breton meets Nadja. On first noticing her in the street, he has little hesitation in approaching her, and henceforth the couple seem scarcely to need to make a rendez-vous when parting since, with uncanny facility, they keep bumping into each other. On one occasion, Nadja is embarrassed at being found by Breton in the Rue de la Chaussée d'Antin, and, as if to forestall the idea that she might have been trailing him, invents the excuse that she has been looking for a sweetshop (p.88). In fact, far from following him, she had intended to avoid showing up at the café where they had a formal appointment later in the day. Breton comes to realize that there is nothing wilful about this crossing of their paths. A day later, he spots Nadja from a taxi and gets out to catch her up in the crowd: 'Voici deux jours consécutifs que je la rencontre: il est clair qu'elle est à ma merci' (p.106) is his somewhat sinister comment.

The final encounter in the book is that between Breton and X, the woman with whom he falls in love. The actual circumstances of this meeting are not described, yet the event is clearly of paramount importance inasmuch as X turns out to be the true object of Breton's surrealist quest. The theme of the encounter, casual at first, may thus be seen to gain in import as the book unfolds, to climax in this final meeting which transcends all that has gone before.

Objective Chance

'Il se peut que la vie demande à être déchiffrée comme un cryptogramme' (p.133). Breton's approach to his enigmatic experiences is cautious and undogmatic. He gathers his data piece by piece, collating what will be the separate pieces of a single puzzle. At first the phenomena seem disparate, unrelated. They come and go in brusque glimmerings, though their brevity does not detract from their insistence on *being noticed*. 'Il s'agit de faits qui [...] présentent chaque fois toutes les apparences d'un signal, sans qu'on puisse dire au juste de quel signal' (p.20), he observes ruefully. Yet the surrealist does make progress: the practice of responding conduces to a sensitivity such that each successive sign is that much more rapidly noticed and construed. The anecdote concerning Breton's presentiment about the BOIS-CHARBONS signs is instructive in this regard: it was not any *individual* sign which made an impression on him but the fact of the *succession* of signs — their insistent recurrence. A sign in isolation may pass unnoticed: a sign which recurs is already more meaningful. And given the tenuousness of the individual sign, it is indeed vital to the project Breton is pursuing that he should seek to consolidate his perceptions — firstly, by recording them (and in due course writing them up in book form); secondly, by grouping them in series or constellations. The practice to which Breton is drawn is one we might call serial perception; and as Sara Tulczyjew writes, 'the important thing is to get the series started' (*67*, p.72).

In schooling himself to recognize patterns of signs, Breton is proceeding along surrealist lines as established in the theory of literary automatism. In the exposition of automatic writing in the 1924 *Manifeste*, the stress lies on the faculty of responding to the verbal flow which emerges from the unconscious levels of the mind. This flow is really nothing other than an associative series — a succession of words whose emergence is largely determined by the words that have emerged previously. I do not need here to engage in a more scrupulous analysis of these associations (sometimes they are semantic, sometimes phonic). What is important is to compare this notion of the poet listening in to the serial flow of language to that of the poet looking out at the succession of signs in the outer world. An exact parallel obtains: the setting of the street is scarcely different from that of the page. Signs float into consciousness in progressively more emphatic series.

Now, it cannot be too firmly stressed that Breton is at pains to avoid elaborating a theoretical framework within which the experiences he relates might be tightly defined. In *Nadja*, he is far more concerned to present the fluidity of experience than to arrest and interpret it. None the less, the reader familiar with *Les Vases communicants* and *L'Amour fou* will inevitably want to test against *Nadja* an important theory enunciated in those later works, namely *hasard objectif* or Objective Chance. One critic, Gisela Steinwachs, states categorically that this later concept is indeed the unspoken generative concept of the work (see *45*, p.81).

Early on in *Nadja*, Breton makes allusion to a strange feeling of 'complicity' with undefined forces, sensed in moments when he might have expected to have sole responsibility for the

running of his life: 'en pleine solitude, je me découvre d'invraisemblables complicités, qui me convainquent de mon illusion
toutes les fois que je me crois seul à la barre du navire' (p.20).
Breton seems to be experiencing the sense of not being fully in
touch with his total personality and hence of being 'haunted' by
an unknown alternative self within his being. The idea can be
seen in terms of the Romantic notion of the double, and I shall
return later to this theme of uncertain identity. For the moment,
though, we may take the above quotation to imply a recognition
of the factor of *chance*. That is to say, Breton's awareness of a
strange hand on the tiller of his existence reflects a subliminal
realization of the role that chance plays in the unfolding of a
man's experience, working not blindly and arbitrarily, but as a
dynamic, intentional force in mysterious collaboration with his
inner being — an *accomplice* by virtue of its willingness to
intervene in the world outside and, so to speak, make things
happen *for him*.

We are now so far advanced as to be able to explain
coincidences in surrealist terms, as the intersection of subjective
and objective lines of development, an intersection facilitated by
what Breton calls Objective Chance. When for instance Breton
is thinking about Nadja in the taxi and then glimpses her on the
crowded pavement, he is experiencing a paradoxical 'determined
coincidence' — something which has all the appearance of a
random event, yet which discloses what Breton later termed 'une
causalité *magique*' (*18*, p.153). While it seems unlikely that one
could subject *Nadja* to statistical analysis, with a view to
estimating the degree of probability of the coincidences
described, the average reader will surely agree that something
improbable and exceptional *is* going on, certainly as far as
Breton's meetings with Nadja are concerned, and that the
explanation of 'blind accident' is inadequate.

The surrealist theory of Objective Chance involves the
recognition of a meaningful relationship between events
occurring within the private space of the psyche and events
taking place in the world of concrete objects and material
circumstance. In positing a correspondence between subjectivity
and objectivity, Breton appears to have adopted Hegel's view

whereby the seemingly arbitrary workings of blind chance are in fact conditioned by systematic dialectical processes through which all phenomena are bound to pass. What Breton was later to define (borrowing terms from an unspecified source, probably a commentary on Hegel) as 'la rencontre d'une causalité externe et d'une finalité interne' (*11*, p.28) may be understood as the fertile intersection of two lines of development — the 'ideal' series nurtured within the subject, and the 'real' series evolving in the world outside.

While the basic terms and shape of this theory derive from Hegelian thought, they are corroborated by a secondary derivation of no less importance. Remarkably consistent with the Hegelian model of the relation of the subject to the outer world is the Freudian model, which can be roughly sketched in terms of the relation of the pleasure principle to the reality principle. Freud's view of this relation was basically one of antagonism, the hopeful wishes of the subjectivity in its search for pleasure being constantly thwarted by the restrictive pressures of objective reality. But Breton adopted the model with a simple reversal, seeing the two principles in terms of reciprocity rather than conflict. Breton's whole conception of *desire* derives directly from this notion of reciprocity, and constitutes a further extension of the theory of Objective Chance.

What was happening when Breton enjoyed those 'invraisemblables complicités' was that his unconscious desire was unusually attuned to his environment. Sitting in a taxi and thinking about Nadja, he unconsciously wishes to meet her again; her materialization on the street is an immediate response to that wish. Converging at an unexpected tangent, the pleasure principle and the reality principle meet, and, in the most compelling yet unpredictable way, a desire is fulfilled. The surrealist notion of desire rests on the view that it is only the superstructures of reason and conscious thought which prevent us from recognizing its ceaseless, purposeful advance at the unconscious level. According to Breton, desire is never at a loss, and will press towards its satisfaction with a tenacity and an ingenuity which are irresistible, not to say ruthless. In *Les Vases communicants*, he will contend that 'l'exigence du désir à la recherche de l'*objet* de sa réalisation dispose étrangement des données extérieures, en tendant égoïstement à ne retenir d'elles que ce qui peut servir à sa cause' (*20*, p.141).

One further concept from a later stage of Breton's thought may usefully be mentioned in this context. In *L'Amour fou*, Breton expounds the notion of the *objet trouvé*, defined as the concrete entity which the subject discovers in the material world and which exactly corresponds to a hitherto unfulfilled wish or unconscious impulse. He adduces the example of the Cinderella Spoon he found at the flea-market, and, drawing on Freudian modes of analysis, demonstrates in close detail how that object symbolically expressed and fulfilled a complex of erotic and emotional associations (see *11*, pp.45-55). I have already referred to a similar fetish presented in *Nadja*, the white half-cylinder in a casket. Writing a decade earlier, Breton was not ready to be explicit, and describes his pleasure only indirectly in terms of the object's belonging to that category of objects which are 'démodés, fragmentés, inutilisables, presque incompréhensibles, pervers enfin au sens où je l'entends et où je l'aime' (p.62). He does go on to allude to a difference between surface and latent meaning, conceding that in fact the thing may well be nothing more than a three-dimensional graph showing the birth-rate in a given Italian town in such and such a year, adding slyly 'ce qui pour cela ne me le rend pas plus lisible' (p.63). In the light of Breton's own Freudian readings of *objets trouvés*, I would suggest that it is quite appropriately 'perverse', i.e. surrealist, to note the shape of this cylinder and the way it fits so snugly inside its velvety container, and to conclude that its latent meaning is that of a representation of coitus — a suggestion which is, moreover, somewhat whimsically consistent with its manifest meaning!

By now it should be clear that we are at liberty to 'read off' meanings from a large proportion of the data listed in *Nadja*, by the simple procedure of applying the conceptual models I have outlined. We can now interpret Breton's elective places as those zones of the city where desire is peculiarly amplified and thus more capable of fulfilment. When Breton walks along the

Boulevard Bonne-Nouvelle, he enters a space in which his unconscious desire is, as it were, mirrored or highlighted. The buildings and objects he comes across represent objective correlatives to his hidden impulses. As material entities, they are not literally part of Breton's mind, and yet each behaves as if it were malleable by the witnessing consciousness in the moment of perception, emerging at that unique point in the sequential unfolding of mental and material experience. Whereupon it functions as a sign that triggers understanding, or at least the excitement which prefigures understanding. As found objects are caught within the sweep of desire, they become tokens of a latent order of meaning, stages in a serial progression towards the revelation of an enhanced relationship between self and environment.

Those perceptual correspondences of which I have spoken may equally be understood as instances of Objective Chance or the symbolic enactment of desire. Each time Breton responds to a shop-sign, he is placing his trust in a logic of non-rational association which engages his emotions and places him in an intimate, libidinal relation to phenomena. Such experiences represent external signals designed to catch the attention of consciousness as precipitates of desire or indices of subliminal intentionality: they are so many visible 'symptoms' of the invisible evolution of the unconscious. The recurrent motifs which form a sort of harmonic sub-system within the Nadja episode are a further instance of a latent continuity underlying what, on the face of it, is a sequence of haphazard events. In one sense, Breton's fascination with eyes is a reflection of his desire to meet a specific woman or type of woman; the reader familiar with the early Breton will agree that he was₁ very much a man keyed up for love, and that his interest in the eyes of passing women reflects a characteristic habit of visual libertinism. Recurrent notations about eyes are thus no more than a straightforward transcription of a more or less conscious desire. From another angle, however, the fact that the imagery of eyes recurs so insistently *after* Breton has met Nadja could be taken as an instance of unconscious signalling from *her* subliminal being.

Many coincidences are explicable in similar terms. A case

might be made for seeing the otherwise trivial coincidence of Nadja showing Breton letters from the misogynous judge as an example of apparently random chance alerting Breton to the ambivalence of his own feelings (as well as of the judge's feelings) towards Nadja. Chance here plays the role of catalyst, drawing to the subject's attention an aspect of reality which he might never have confronted for himself. Likewise, the incident where Breton receives a coded message that the communion kiss he has shared with Nadja is likely to be profaned, represents a powerful spotlight on the relationship. It is as though Breton's unconscious mind were lunging out at an external object — Aragon's postcard — which will exactly articulate a thought which consciousness is seeking to repress, namely, that his attitude to Nadja is neither pure nor reverent.

My final category of the encounter simply represents the most dramatic enactment of Objective Chance. The way Breton bumps into Nadja is, as I have suggested, a manifestation of the collision of subjective desire with material object, the pleasure principle harmonizing with the reality principle. The encounter with X can be read straightforwardly as the climax of this series. As Breton later remarked of the surrealist quest for revelation within the city, 'la rencontre imprévue qui tend toujours, explicitement ou non, à prendre les traits d'une femme, marque la culmination de cette quête' (*15*, p.135).

Prospecting the self

The act of noticing a sign in external reality must imply a relationship between subject and thing perceived. Moreover, the act of making sense of the sign will necessarily involve the subject in a decision about interpretation such that the thing perceived emerges into meaning in a way dependent on the subject's attitude. If an awareness of viewpoints is necessary for one to appreciate the shift from MAISON ROUGE to POLICE, so the data collected in *Nadja* may offer the reader a way of intuitively assessing the *angle* at which Breton looks out on to experience at large.

It is of course important to the effect of documentary

completeness in *Nadja* that Breton should be at pains to specify
the details of which street he happened to be walking along,
which book he bought, which person he bumped into. Yet, in
another sense, what really matters is not so much the specific
objects of attention as the circumstance of attention itself.
Breton is less preoccupied with, say, the actual blue glove which
a woman friend offers to leave at the Centrale surréaliste than
with the emotional associations which flood his sensibility: 'Je
ne sais ce qu'alors il put y avoir pour moi de redoutablement, de
merveilleusement décisif dans la pensée de ce gant quittant pour
toujours cette main' (p.65). The meaning of the anecdote is
grounded in the connection between subject and sign, not in the
sign on its own; indeed, a definition of the 'surrealist sign'
would surely need to tie meaning precisely to this notion of a
linking relationship.

We are now considering *Nadja* as an experience of reading in
which what the reader witnesses is what Breton witnesses, and
above all the *way* in which he witnesses those things. In this
sense, *Nadja* is predominantly a record of the transactions of a
certain subject responding to the objective world. Added to this
is the more or less explicit way in which Breton informs his
reader that what he is showing him are not just any old
sensations, but 'sensations électives' (p.22): in other words,
Breton is selecting, and thereby giving special status to, those
striking data which appear relevant to his personal project. This
last, we now realize, is essentially an autobiographical one.

The text in fact initiates the theme of self-prospection in its
opening motto-question 'Qui suis-je?' (p.9), and pursues the
problem through the succeeding pages. Breton is looking for
himself, and when he gives way to experience apparently outside
the realm of subjectivity, it is precisely because he is groping for
signposts to help him locate that realm. In search of something
fleeting and fragile — 'cette image la plus fugace et la plus
alertée de moi-même' (p.43) — he is concerned to delineate a
self-portrait with a difference. For whereas in traditional autobiography, the authorial camera is, so to speak, aimed *by* the
subject *at* the subject, Breton's strategy is to point his camera
outwards, at that which is *other than himself*.

At a late stage in the book, Breton abruptly introduces a curious list of images which are given without explanation, like some glittering riddle. What are we to make of these lyrical references to the lustre of rare metals when sawn open, the phosphorescence of quarries and wells, the crackling of a wooden clock tossed on a bonfire while striking the hour, the multiform representation of a single couple in a painting by Watteau, the stately beauty of reservoirs or of the walls of houses under demolition? All these things, we are darkly informed, are relevant to Breton's project of self-definition: 'Rien de tout cela, rien de ce qui constitue pour moi ma lumière propre, n'a été oublié' (p.128).

The claim makes more sense when read in conjunction with an earlier statement in which the individual sensibility or temperament is defined in terms of 'les dispositions d'un esprit à l'égard de certaines choses' (p.16). In a discussion of the paintings of De Chirico, Breton alludes to the eccentric juxtaposition of objects therein, and whimsically suggests that a full report on the artist's intimate views concerning artichokes, gloves, biscuits and cotton-reels would afford us penetrating insights into the nature of his creativity (p.15). We may infer that, in *Nadja*, Breton is offering us just such a dossier. Self-prospection here takes the form of a logbook which tabulates the subject's encounter with a series of absorbing things outside itself, and thereby registers Breton's unique 'way of being', i.e. his idiosyncratic self, as a kind of contour or imprint left by the characteristic motions of his 'way of seeing'.

In saying this, I am shifting my own angle of vision upon Breton's inventory of signs. My point now is that, in the long run, Breton is less intent on illuminating an 'objective' surreality valid for other people, than on mapping the manifestations of the surreal as so many illuminations of his own personality. The task of deciphering the cryptogram of life thus turns out to be co-extensive with (if not overtaken by) the task of deciphering the cryptogram of identity.

Just now I used the image of the camera as a means to characterize Breton's autobiographical practice. But the reader of *Nadja* will know that such a casual use of the metaphor of photography cannot be innocent: the book is too overtly pictorial for us to ignore Breton's actual photographic evidence. The document most crucial to the present discussion is obviously the studio portrait of Breton himself, which he appears to have had taken by a professional photographer, in December 1927 or thereabouts, for inclusion in the first edition of *Nadja* a few months later. The last illustration in that edition, it shows a serious man in his early thirties, hair slicked back and tie neatly tied; the head is lit carefully from above, and the calm expression on the face is suggestive of self-assurance and ambitiousness. None the less, the photo has an unsettling effect. Thus far, Breton has deliberately avoided showing himself except indirectly, in the ways I have discussed. Suddenly to throw into the text an irrefutable index of his identity — a photo which could be used for an identity card — is a brutal revocation of the principle of obliqueness. It comes across as a truculent, even a pathetic gesture, especially since Breton's text at this juncture is lamenting the limitations of writing: the caption to the illustration cites the depressing phrase 'J'envie (c'est une façon de parler) tout homme qui a le temps de préparer quelque chose comme un livre' (p.173). This apparent loss of heart brings matters to a head, and I feel that, instead of clarifying Breton's personality, the photo poses the problem of identity in its most uncompromising form. 'Qui suis-je?' Who is this man? Can we ever know him, *even if* he shows his face? Is he not too posed, too aloof, to be truly open to our gaze? There can be no short-cut to revelation. The photo must be a disappointment.

Given that so many other minor participants in the narrative are honoured with full-page portraits, it is surprising to find that the heroine of the book is treated in a quite aberrant way. Rather than give a normal full-face portrait of Nadja, Breton has devised (or, at the very least, has had a friend devise to his instructions) a photomontage in the form of a fourfold repetition of a single band cut from a photograph of Nadja and showing only her eyes and forehead. I shall return later to the implications of this bizarre way of showing Nadja while equally not showing her; for the moment, we may simply infer that Breton is signalling to us that the woman's identity is especially problematic.

What has not yet been said of the operation of self-prospection in *Nadja* is that it is an anguished one. 'Qui suis-je?' is no idle query, but a metaphysical wail. And if Breton should have the confidence to pursue himself, he lacks the certainty of being able to catch up with the same person. In a joke which he tells with glacial seriousness at the close of the book, an amnesiac called Monsieur Delouit is described as arriving at a hotel and asking the clerk to repeat his room number: having gone up to his room, he jumps out of the window and comes in again at the front entrance, once more asking the clerk to call out his number (pp.183-84). One way of understanding the joke is as a comment on the theme of vacillating identity (cf. *44*, pp.52-56). A complementary one is that it is a sardonic meditation on suicide, or the extinction of identity. In an earlier passage, Breton tells us the story of Eluard mistaking him for a dead friend (p.29). A little later, he refers to Robert Desnos's claim to have taken on the personality of Marcel Duchamp, by that time resident in America (p.35). Nadja is repeatedly described as mimicking historical or mythological figures such as Madame de Chevreuse (p.127) and Mélusine (pp.125 and 149/55). Such transferences of identity surely create undercurrents of uncertainty for Breton. Who am I? If I can list all those objective facts I have witnessed from my unique viewpoint, those elective signs lit by my 'lumière propre', will I not then see my true being reflected in them? Do I not become a meaningful subject in relation to those things, and does not their sum reflect my singularity, my specificity?

So far, the answer to these questions has been positive. Yes, one can, broadly speaking, deduce a single sensibility from the sweep of Breton's writings (see *54*). But in the strict context of *Nadja*, Breton does not really seem so sure of a positive answer. In the final analysis he fails to fix on a single compelling position from which we might measure his angle of vision. When he speaks of Watteau's painting simultaneously depicting the same couple several times over, is he not seeing in the picture a symbolic presentation of multiple identity? What of the thriller film in which a single Chinaman invades New York in the form of thousands of replicas of himself (p.38)? Underlying the drolleries of the Delouit joke is the suggestion that the self is something unreliable, de-centred. Thanks to Breton's anxious hints at this theme, the book begins to lose its univocal fixity. How could it indeed remain stable, since Breton is shifting his stance all the time, being now critic, now lover, now hunter of the surreal, now helpless victim of chance and emotion?

The portrait of Breton beginning to emerge is one of a fluc-tuating, random collocation of attitudes and impulses, some-thing totally remote from what we customarily conceive of as the stable, specific identity of a human being. (This very notion is, incidentally, developed at length in a passage in Breton's poem 'Les Etats généraux'; see *19*, p.67.) When, on the first page of *Nadja*, Breton tries to describe the eerie feelings he is having about himself, he introduces the image of a phantom, suggesting firstly that he is a mere ghost treading in the footsteps of a long-dead former personality. But then he corrects himself, and makes things even worse: he now sees the phantom as the true self, of which the apparently 'normal' self is merely the faltering double (pp.9-10).

From such images and elliptic conjectures, we may deduce a Bretonian model of personality. It is dual in nature. A human being has a public persona, ratified by consciousness, the reasoning faculty and the will. But more important is the phantom in the background — the subliminal self, composed of latent desires, poetic impulses and instinctual reflexes. The true centre of one's being lies there, in the darkness. Michel Carrouges write that

> le fantôme qui est dessiné en filigrane à chaque page de *Nadja* devient le symbole troublant du moi le plus secret, du narcissisme, du double, des puissances nocturnes, de l'âme, de la mort, de l'immortalité, de l'au-delà, bref de tout ce que vous aviez coutume de chasser de votre pensée.
> (*57*, p.223)

Thus, below the surface of routine existence, strange and com-pelling forces come into play. Breton's exploration of surreality and the self now takes on a more tense keynote. He is not so much working towards a clarification of what he terms the 'organic plane' of existence as edging in trepidation into 'un monde comme défendu' (p.19), a domain of mystery and terror. When Nadja one day looks into his eyes and suddenly blinks emphatically, as if having recognized him — or something within him — across a great distance (p.90), it is as though she has recognized that subliminal self which is so painfully *other* than Breton the Parisian stroller, the surrealist theorist, the man in the studio portrait.

I want next to argue that *Nadja* is shot through with evidence of Breton's panic responses. Again and again, there are signs that Breton's world-picture is not really so secure, supported by comforting notions of Objective Chance and the like. There is a strong case for reading his book as the record of a man's disquieting discovery that the world is gripped in the thrall of paranormal forces.

Dark powers

The conception of an alternative reality or 'surreality' — or more accurately, an alternative way of viewing existing reality — is intimately bound up with the question of the paranormal. Among the formative experiences in Breton's evolution as a poet was the discovery that he could visualize images from Rimbaud's *Illuminations* and project them onto his concrete environment. In *Nadja*, he insists on the literal force of Rimbaud's 'pouvoir d'incantation' (p.59), so compelling that houses and gardens on the outskirts of Nantes were fantastically transformed. The hallucinatory episode of the BOIS-CHARBONS signs, linked as it is with the prior occurrence of that phrase in an automatic text, may be read as a further instance of paranormal phenomena stimulated by the poetic word. And the capacity of the automatic flow to institute itself in material form is finally demonstrated when Breton discovers that a passage from his *Poisson soluble*, composed in 1923, represents an uncanny anticipation of Nadja's entry into his life in 1926 (see pp.92-93).

The notion of a correspondence between language and

material events had been a preoccupation of the surrealists some
years before Nadja's arrival. During the *époque des sommeils* of
late 1922, briefly mentioned in *Nadja* (p.35) and described in
detail in Aragon's *Une Vague de rêves* (1924), the group's
experiments in automatic writing had led to startling results, the
free dictation of the unconscious prompting several poets to
experience spectacular forms of hallucination. Robert Desnos in
particular specialized in prophetic utterances made while in a
state of trance, and Breton speaks admiringly of their 'valeur
absolue d'oracle' (p.36).

Nadja herself is the person who most impressively reveals the
dark powers to which Breton is so clearly drawn. She claims to
guess the direction of an underground passage near the Palais de
Justice (p.94), and to be able to divine the thoughts of workers
on the train (p.77). During only her second conversation with
Breton, she guesses correctly that his wife is a brunette, and that
they have a dog and a cat (p.85). And when Nadja visits Breton's
study, she is able to sense the presence of a pair of horns on a
New Guinea mask hidden inside a cabinet (p.146).

No doubt there is an element of mystification in some of these
episodes. One cannot take Nadja too seriously when she seizes
Breton's hat to look at the initials on the inside, telling him that
she does this regularly to determine the nationality of her com-
panions (p.88)! On the other hand, there seems little likelihood
that Nadja is merely play-acting when she insists that there is a
hand gleaming over the Seine one evening (p.98), or when she
hears voices whispering to her (pp.97 and 107). That she herself
recognizes the difference between sham hallucination and the
real thing is made clear in the episode of the train journey she
takes with Breton to Saint-Germain, when she clearly sees a man
peering into their carriage, suspended upside down from the
roof of the train. 'Je te dis qu'il est là, il a une casquette', she
exclaims. 'Non ce n'est pas une vision' (p.126). The narrative
goes on to reveal Breton's own complicity in the matter. Twice
he looks out in sceptical mood, but the second time, he glimpses
a railway employee in a cap (pp.126-27).[1] Is there 'really' a man

---

[1] Though Breton does not make the connection, it is remarkable that this
incident enacts the very first sentence he obtained as the model of the automatic
utterance: 'Il y a un homme coupé en deux par la fenêtre' (see *16*, pp.31 ff.).

on the roof? Or is Breton simply acceding to his companion's intensity of conviction, joining in her delusion? Such unanswerable questions only compound the excitement.

Another invitation to see in Nadja a woman gifted with paranormal powers is voiced in a passage which draws a parallel between her and the celebrated medium Helen Smith (p.93; see also *15*, p.138). The latter claimed to be in telepathic contact with the inhabitants of Mars, and, while in a state of trance, to write at length in Martian language. The psychologist Théodore Flournoy, who investigated her case, came to the conclusion that Helen Smith was remarkable because she had gained special access not to the supernatural but to her own unconscious mind. Given that the surrealists were never interested in Spiritualist beliefs in a spirit realm outside the scope of earthly existence, they were delighted with this confirmation of their belief in the powers of the non-rational faculties.

The important association here is that between subliminal powers and verbal fluency. Breton seems to have seen a second Desnos in Nadja, whose utterances and writings are cited with unconcealed emotion. On their very first meeting, she treats Breton to some of this verbal magic, with such statements as: 'Vous ne pouviez manquer d'arriver à cette étoile. [...] elle est comme le cœur d'une fleur sans cœur' (p.81). As an allusion to his supposed destiny, this cuts Breton to the quick; with hindsight, the reader might take it as a prediction of his eventual 'heartlessness' with regard to the girl.

At this time, Breton was perfectly familiar with fortune-telling and allied practices. He had expressed his admiration for clairvoyants in at least two major texts, 'Entrée des médiums' (1922) and 'Lettre aux voyantes' (1925). In common with his friends, he used regularly to consult Madame Sacco, a Parisian fortuneteller. When Breton asks Max Ernst if he will paint a portrait of Nadja, Ernst consults Madame Sacco, only to receive a firm warning not to do so (p.124). Breton at once applauds Ernst's refusal.

Much of this may seem like superstitious nonsense. What is undeniable is that Breton has taken steps to communicate his responses to paranormal events in an earnest and convincing manner. Sometimes he is aware that he may seem gullible, as when he speaks of Nadja's prediction that a window will turn red and adds parenthetically: '(Je regrette, mais je n'y puis rien, que ceci passe peut-être les limites de la crédibilité. Cependant, à pareil sujet, je m'en voudrais de prendre parti: je me borne à *convenir* que de noire, cette fenêtre est alors devenue rouge, c'est tout.)' (p.96). All the same, the fact that he then goes on to admit to a sense of fear is surely an unequivocal hint that there was *something* happening which he felt to be more than illusion or mystification. Indeed one might put the point more sharply and say that Breton not only contends that something paranormal *was* happening, he actually treats the sensation of fear as his objective guarantee that he is indeed in the compelling presence of the dark powers.

A risky vocation

If *Nadja* is a book about the sporadic irruption of fantastic events within a predictable world, we may locate the crux of its message in a distinction between two sorts of experience, corresponding to two sorts of emotion: routine living, which gives rise to boredom, and adventurous living, which gives rise to exhilaration.

Breton is keen to emphasize his personal propensity to be bored, using language reminiscent of Baudelaire to castigate the 'sempiternelle vie' (p.130) from which he evidently wants to escape. Once Nadja has disappeared, he lapses from excitement into depression, referring to the external world as 'cette histoire à dormir debout' (p.180) and contrasting it with the preceding adventure. Yet the dejection which plagues Breton is very much an 'ennui vibrant' (p.16), a negative condition which somehow manages to conduce to its opposite. When Breton trails along the Boulevard Bonne-Nouvelle, or when, on 4 October 1926, he strolls along the Rue Lafayette 'à la fin d'un de ces après-midi tout à fait désœuvrés et très mornes, comme j'ai le secret d'en passer' (p.71), he is acting the part of the listless Baudelairian *flâneur*, with the difference that he is on the lookout for some sudden disruption of the monochrome surface of life. His torpor is, effectively, the negative precondition of surrealist intensity.

There is a distinct tone of voice which accompanies each expression of Breton's desire to step out of the humdrum. Those startling coincidences and encounters, those deliriums and hypnotic reflexes, those abrupt cracks in the façade of routine, all are linked by the common denominator of Breton's emotional response. Earlier, I suggested that Objective Chance is the principle which may be said to generate the episodes in question. I next suggested that they might equally be meaningful to Breton as ways of finding himself. Now I would propose that a way of deciphering these disparate events might be to see them all as symptomatic of a special state of poetic arousal in which the dominant factor is a feeling of panic — of losing oneself, rather than finding oneself!

Scanning the book once more with this in mind, we find many unmistakable indices of anxiety and even terror. I have already mentioned that Breton reacts in a scared way to such incidents as Nadja's prediction about the red window, the BOIS-CHARBONS episode, the proposed gift of a blue glove. He feels ill at ease about statues; he is upset by paintings by Uccello and De Chirico, just as Nadja is upset by a poem by Alfred Jarry: '(Avec effroi, fermant le livre): "Oh! ceci, c'est la mort!"' (p.84). After thinking about the disquieting play *Les Détraquées*, Breton has a nightmare about a huge green insect (p.57). His book closes with a news cutting about an aeroplane lost at sea whose last radio message reads like a grim understatement of total despair: 'Il y a quelque chose qui ne va pas' (p.190).

The many references to night consolidate this panicky yet somehow alluring mood. Breton muses on the outcome of a hypothetical encounter with a naked woman in a wood by night (p.44), and seems keen to accompany Nadja on a nocturnal excursion to the forest at Le Vésinet (p.126). It is as though nocturnal existence were synonymous with non-rational behaviour, an abandonment of constraint — a time of wild possibility and adventure. The dominant image of the phantom, with which the book opens, is associated with nocturnal apparitions, and is echoed in a later reference to a man entering a museum stealthily by night in order to gaze at a woman's portrait by lamplight (p.132) — an allusion which makes little sense until read as a coded statement of the surrealist association of love and risk. Finally, Breton's allegiance to the powers of darkness is proclaimed in his wish to be a creature of the night (i.e. of the irrational) rather than of the day (i.e. of the commonsensical): 'Je préfère, encore une fois, marcher dans la nuit à me croire celui qui marche dans le jour' (p.69).

It is now still possible to envisage *Nadja* as a book crammed with signs, but this time with a shift in emphasis on the notion of *sign*. Pierre Albouy offers a perceptive distinction here, by using the term *sign* to denote simply an event or message which the observer is at liberty to notice or ignore and the term *signal* to denote the event or message which the observer is unable to bypass: 'Le signe demande à être traduit, le signal, à être obéi', he writes (*21*, p.237).

Breton is indeed subjected to a good many signals in the book, and acknowledges them as 'sollicitations perpétuelles' (p.17) impossible to ignore. The strength of the signal is especially manifest in the illustrations, which bristle with words in imperious capitals on shop-fronts, posters, signposts and so forth. To scan these is to read off a coded telegram demanding immediate action:

HOTEL DES GRANDS HOMMES/ BOIS CHARBONS/ L'ETREINTE DE LA PIEUVRE/ TROISIEME DIALOGUE/ CAMEES DURS/ SPHINX HOTEL/ MAZDA/ LES AUBES.

The placing of an innocuous photograph of the Humanité bookshop opposite the opening page of the Nadja episode is surely not accidental, and suggests that Breton was aware of a possible secondary meaning attaching to the boldly lettered placard above the shop: ON SIGNE ICI, with accompanying arrow (p.70). In all probability the manager of the Humanité bookshop intended a simple primary meaning such as 'This is the place to sign on as a member of the Communist Party'. But Breton's book is persuasive at lower levels than the commonsensical, and I would suggest that this illustration provides a perfect frontispiece for the ensuing narrative, which is all about Breton being forced to take note of the signals released or brought into focus by Nadja. The phrase and the arrow are emblematic of an urgency, an insistence that goes beyond an invitation.

Thus if Breton is being required to notice and to record, he is also being required to take action on his own account, to intervene, to commit himself to an operation lying outside his customary orbit. Moreover, Breton seems keen to establish himself in the role of the poet always heroically on the alert. One senses an element of pride when he claims to be ready to keep any appointment made by Desnos in a state of trance (p.36), or when he speaks of his unequivocal response on meeting Nadja: 'Sans hésitation j'adresse la parole à l'inconnue' (p.73). Unreflecting obedience to the signal emerges as a surrealist absolute.

In a moment of speculation midway in his dealings with Nadja, Breton recognizes the gravity of the challenge she has laid down. To follow her is to respond to an implicit command, to contest which would mean forfeiting all chance of knowing the secrets to which she can lead: 'Que faire tantôt, si je ne la vois pas? Et si je ne la voyais plus? Je ne *saurais* plus. J'aurais donc mérité de ne plus savoir. Et cela ne se retrouverait jamais' (p.105). The imperative of the 'all or nothing' gamble emerges plainly. And yet the book makes it very clear that the gamble is no soft option. Surrealist spontaneity is not so easy. The text 'L'Esprit nouveau', which Breton shows Nadja, concerns the sighting of an unknown woman in the Rue Bonaparte a few years earlier; though impressed by her demeanour, Breton chooses first to consult two friends who had also seen her. By the time they decide to track her down, it is too late: the woman has vanished (see *17*, pp.101-03). While driving in Nantes one day, Breton exchanges an exciting glance with a working-class woman, but stupidly fails to stop (p.33). Breton was a great admirer of the actress Blanche Derval, who so impressed him in the part of Solange in *Les Détraquées*: years later he reproaches himself for having failed to find out what she was like as a real person off-stage (p.55). The climax of his affair with Nadja is described in a decisive footnote, to which I shall return. Driving

back from Versailles one evening with Nadja as passenger, he
encounters the absolute challenge of *amour fou*: Nadja presses
her foot over his upon the accelerator, and with her hands over
his eyes, seeks to engage him in what could only be a fatal
embrace. Breton disengages himself, and the incident is closed.
None the less, he broods upon it, and the footnote (the longest in
the whole book, taking up practically a whole page of text)
represents a curious attempt to disculpate himself from the
charge of self-preservation. Breton seeks an excuse for not
having risked all on a kiss by stating that he did not love Nadja
enough; then he goes on to acknowledge her gesture as totally
admirable, a triumphant denial of all trivial considerations. He
would, he claims, *ideally* love to emulate such commitment:
'Idéalement au moins je me retrouve souvent, les yeux bandés,
au volant de cette voiture sauvage' (p.179).

The incident brings out clearly the element of caution which
inhibits Breton's complete surrender to the forces which beckon
to him. The instinct of self-preservation can, he admits, make us
draw back from certain disturbing conjunctions of circumstance
(p.21). The *faits-glissades* may give pleasure, but the *faits-
précipices* can conduce to vertigo and dread. The missed oppor-
tunities which, to his credit, he outlines as all part of the story
are illuminating in that they plot the exact *limits* of Breton's
availability to the surrealist adventure. Conversely, what is so
striking about Nadja is that she seems to have no reflexes of self-
preservation, and launches herself wholeheartedly into life at
each moment, oblivious of risk. 'Je sais que ce *départ*, pour
Nadja, d'un point où il est déjà si rare, si téméraire de vouloir
arriver, s'effectuait au mépris de tout ce qu'il est convenu
d'invoquer au moment où l'on se perd, très loin volontairement
du dernier radeau' (p.132). Breton's undoubted admiration is
modified by a certain reserve. He is perhaps just bold enough
himself to reach the point from which Nadja has already dared
advance into yet further reaches of passionate risk. In her world,
Breton remarks elsewhere, 'tout prenait si vite l'apparence de la
montée et de la chute' (p.159). That is, the precipitous nature of
genuine surrealist experience is such that headlong plunging can
swiftly follow upon an exhilarating ascent.

Though one may have doubts about his courage, one should at least credit Breton with the ability to define the surrealist ambition. The following flamboyant statement represents perhaps an ideal rather than an actual posture, yet it does none the less convey the attractiveness of surrealist *disponibilité*:

> Que la grande inconscience vive et sonore qui m'inspire mes seuls actes probants dispose à tout jamais de tout ce qui est moi. [...] Je ne veux encore une fois reconnaître qu'elle, je veux ne compter que sur elle et presque à loisir parcourir ses jetées immenses, fixant moi-même un point brillant que je sais être dans mon œil et qui m'épargne de me heurter à ses ballots de nuit. (p.183)

The central tenet articulated in this prayer-like passage is that of availability to the dictates of the irrational — in other words, to desire or to Objective Chance. That Breton comes up with an image of himself roaming over jetties in an apparently marine setting is a curious echo of the imagery of shipwreck and the 'dernier radeau' mentioned a moment ago. The allusion to night is by now a familiar association. The bright point which seems to guide him, like a lighthouse in the dark ocean, is somewhat paradoxically located in his own eye. The suggestion appears to be that Breton hopes to exercise some degree of conscious control over his recklessness. Does he expect this margin of safety to preserve him from disaster?

I have now opened up a perspective whereby the initial query as to Breton's identity may be seen to modulate into a query about his poetic vocation. In the opening pages of *Nadja* he does indeed explicitly ask not only *who* he is, but *what* it is that he has been designated to achieve. The compendium of signs which reflects a sensibility is, in the first instance, a means to plot the co-ordinates of self. At a secondary stage, the realization of how he differs from other people will in turn define a vocation:

> N'est-ce pas dans la mesure exacte où je prendrai con-science de cette différenciation que je me révélerai ce

qu'entre tous les autres je suis venu faire en ce monde et de
quel message unique je suis porteur pour ne pouvoir
répondre de son sort que sur ma tête? (p.11)

The idea of a message so vital that the messenger must guard it
with his very life reminds us that danger is of the essence. The
enterprise in which the surrealist is engaged is not the making of
literature, but the prospection of those aspects of real-life
experience which have an urgent bearing on his inner being. In
complying with the signals of chance, the poet commits himself
to a path which leads beyond the secure confines of routine and
into unmapped territory. Surrealism is a risky adventure, it
seems, and yet if there were no risk, there would be no adventure
— and no prizes.

Danger is thus the touchstone of Breton's surrealist honour.
Without it, nothing may be gained. And though Breton may
falter when the highest challenge occurs, it is not for lack of a
will to expose himself. Fear is indeed a measure of the gravity of
the experience. Surrealist availability means, precisely,
remaining off guard, off balance, 'far from the last life-raft'. It
is in this sense that Breton's encounter with Nadja takes on the
character of a moral challenge. Entering his life after a sequence
of like encounters from which he had shied away, she represents
for Breton the ultimate test of his capacity to rise 'à la hauteur
de l'intention surréaliste' (*16*, p.89).

3. The Quest for Values

The impact of Nadja

'C'est à une puissance extrême de défi que certains êtres très rares qui peuvent les uns des autres tout attendre et tout craindre se reconnaîtront toujours' (p.179). Breton's admiration for Nadja is immediate and unconcealed, and shines through in his choice of title for the book. None the less, as the text progresses, so does Nadja's prestige slowly wane. As a rare creature with an unmistakable 'puissance extrême de défi', she invites Breton to expect an immense amount. Yet, at the same time, she gives him occasion to contemplate the reverse side of that invitation. 'Tout attendre' is counterbalanced by 'tout craindre'. The positive and negative aspects of their relationship are indeed perceptible from the outset, and this fatal dualism lies at the very heart of the book.

Let us first examine the positive features of this surrealist heroine, of whom Breton was still prepared, in 1952, to speak with fervour as 'une magicienne [...] faite pour centrer sur elle tout l'appétit du merveilleux' (*15*, p.138). Seen in purely surrealist terms, Nadja is someone who lives out all the poetic principles: capricious spontaneity, irrational creativity, uncompromising defiance of convention. A model example of how to escape from the loathsome prison of logic (see p.169), she is the very epitome of surrealist ideology and the perfect medium of the surreal.

It is evident that Breton is concerned to accentuate his portrayal of Nadja as a creature of irresistible allurement. The opening description of her appearance — walking alone, her eyes made-up in a dissonant way, her head held high, light-footed, the hint of a smile at her lips — is offered not just as objective fact, but as moral persuasion. This is the Encounter of Encounters, the long-awaited arrival of the answer to Breton's questions. Small wonder that he indulges in eager hyperbole and begins to idealize Nadja as a being who transcends all human limitations: 'elle est pure, libre de tout lien terrestre' (p.104). Or again: 'J'ai pris, du premier au dernier jour, Nadja pour un génie libre, quelque chose comme un de ces esprits de l'air que certaines pratiques de magie permettent momentanément de s'attacher, mais qu'il ne saurait être question de se soumettre' (p.130).

However, Nadja is more complicated than this, as Breton eventually has to acknowledge. While her role as guide to the surreal gives rise to such fantastic gestures as dressing up like the devil or the mythical Mélusine, she also exhibits other, less poetic features. For, despite Breton's idealizations, Nadja is a creature of flesh and blood — a woman with physical and emotional needs, reacting to the specific conditions of Paris in 1926 and to the real-life influence of Breton as a man. Breton's journal of their time together is fascinating above all in its almost involuntary disclosures of qualities which compromise her status as exemplary surrealist.

Whereas Nadja may look splendidly theatrical in the street, this cannot disguise the fact that her existence is anything but splendid. She is physically frail, and her thin dress makes her shiver; she has a history of disease (presumably tubercular) but lacks the money for a cure (p.80). There are hints of a period of drug-addiction, of an illegitimate child, of occasional prostitution, of a succession of older lovers. She comes from a decent working-class home in the provinces and seeks clumsily to reassure her mother that she is living honourably in the capital (pp.76-77). Yet she is prepared to flirt indiscriminately with men in public places and to collect love letters from all and sundry. She spends her money carelessly, though she has no income. She is at times a chatterbox, amusing herself with facile talk and song, often making scenes in public just for the fun of it. She has no aim in life, and the poetic slogan 'Je suis l'âme errante' (p.82) which she offers when Breton asks who she really is, might just as well be idle mystification, an embellishment of the brute fact that she is an aimless social drop-out.

Breton is much vexed by this reverse side of his ideal. Nadja embarrasses him by her silliness, her prattling. Surely she knows better, he begins to ask. In the latter stages of the narrative, he muses more and more on the discrepancy between the Nadja of his vision and the Nadja who lapses into disastrous mediocrity.

> Qui est la vraie Nadja [...] — je veux dire de la créature toujours inspirée et inspirante qui n'aimait qu'être dans la rue, pour elle seul champ d'expérience valable, dans la rue, à portée d'interrogation de tout être humain lancé sur une grande chimère, ou (pourquoi ne pas le reconnaître?) de celle qui *tombait*, parfois, parce qu'enfin d'autres s'étaient crus autorisés à lui adresser la parole, n'avaient su voir en elle que la plus pauvre de toutes les femmes et de toutes la plus mal défendue? (pp.133-34)

The issue is brought to a head by Breton's allusion to the street as Nadja's natural element. On the one hand, this is the space of surrealist possibility, the realm of Objective Chance and of poetic revelation; in short, the place where 'certain rare beings' may expect to meet and to enjoy unusual experiences. On the one hand, the streets of Paris are also a place for prostitution. The status of Nadja as pure surrealist woman is, apparently, highly tenuous, since it would seem that it takes only one *inappropriate* approach — a man coming up to make a sexual proposition — for her surrealist purity to lapse, for the *magicienne* to be reduced to a mere *péripatéticienne*. Breton is bemused by this dualism, and by Nadja's incapacity fully to assume what he evidently sees as her surrealist calling. She is, as Breton eventually concedes 'forte, enfin, et très faible, comme on peut l'être, de cette idée qui toujours avait été la sienne' (p.168). That is, she grasps the fundamental surrealist proposition that man must seek to live in freedom, but fails to realize that this principle is too demanding to be applied all the time. Her genius is simply not discriminatory, as is evidenced, for Breton, in her inability to distinguish between her own most trite and most inspired utterances (p.157). She is, in a sense, incapable of managing her genius, and the awful realization dawns on Breton that he cannot help her to assume her destiny as Surrealist Woman, since she is too prone to the other demands on her personality. A tragic momentum builds up, as Breton finally sees, hastened by his own resistance to these facts.

There comes a point where Breton begins to reveal human inadequacies that belie his surrealist pretensions. When Nadja tells him one day about being slapped in the face by a man in a café, he draws back in horror, unable to accept this contamination of his idealized image. He admits as much in the following passage, in which the split between the two sides of Nadja's existence is clearly articulated:

> Emerveillé que je continuais à être par cette manière de se diriger ne se fondant que sur la plus pure intuition et tenant sans cesse du prodige, j'étais aussi de plus en plus alarmé de sentir que, lorsque je la quittais, elle était reprise par le tourbillon de cette vie se poursuivant en dehors d'elle, acharnée à obtenir d'elle, entre autres concessions, qu'elle mangeât, qu'elle dormît. (p.136)

Here we see Breton vainly trying to reduce the shortcomings of Nadja's existence to simple problems of cash (he apparently does give her financial help, there being reference to a gift of 1500 francs on 9 October: see p.111). But what is really at issue is not that Nadja is poor, but that her propensity for surrealist spontaneity is indissociable from vulnerability before material circumstance.

If it is true that it is Breton's idiosyncratic perspective on Nadja which highlights the contradiction in her nature, it is equally true that a resolution is available (if that is an admissible term) to Breton, namely: to fall in love with Nadja. Love could, he concedes, have accomplished the miracle, bringing Nadja into a viable relationship with everyday existence while sustaining her in her surrealist calling. 'Seul l'amour au sens où je l'entends — mais alors le mystérieux, l'improbable, l'unique, le confondant et l'indubitable amour — tel enfin qu'il ne peut être qu'à toute épreuve, eût pu permettre ici l'accomplissement du miracle', he somewhat pompously observes (p.159). As becomes evident in the last section of the book, love of the kind defined here was to be possible only with a different woman.

It is surely undeniable that Breton sought to enter into an amorous relationship with Nadja. His initial advances are hardly those of an impartial observer. How could they be, when Breton insists all along on emotional involvement as the key to any adventure? Their long walks in the streets, their nocturnal visit to the Tuileries, their intimate conversations in restaurants, are all consistent with the behaviour of lovers. Breton twice mentions kissing Nadja (pp.92 and 108), albeit with a hint each time about the menacing atmosphere of the embrace. When the couple leave town by train late on the evening of 12 October, there is a clear presupposition of physical intimacy, even though the events of the night are not spelled out.

Speaking at a later date about all this, Breton can say nothing more than that true love simply did not happen. 'Toutes les séductions qu'elle exerce sur moi restent d'ordre intellectuel, ne se résolvent pas en amour' (*15*, p.138). In the course of his immediate ruminations on the problem, he points out how ill-suited they are, in that they are unable to agree about the simplest facts of existence (p.157) — an assertion which falls a little flat coming from a champion of non-conformity! He recognizes that he must have appeared 'black and cold' towards Nadja, and admits feeling anger instead of pity when she tells tales of the indignities she has suffered (pp.130 and 134). Speaking of the relationship after its collapse, he surmises — with embarrassed caution, as witness the double use of *peut-être* — that he was simply inadequate in face of the challenge she represented: 'Quelque envie que j'en ai[e] eue, quelque illusion peut-être aussi, je n'ai peut-être pas été à la hauteur de ce qu'elle me proposait. Mais que me proposait-elle?' (p.159). To which we might answer, simply love, rather than some promise of poetic revelation which Breton seems to be trying to smuggle into his sentence, as a means to conceal his emotional impotence.

Nadja, conversely, does fall in love with Breton. On only the second day of the relationship, she acknowledges his magnetism, even his dominion.

Elle me parle maintenant de mon pouvoir sur elle, de la
faculté que j'ai de lui faire penser et faire ce que je veux,
peut-être plus que je ne crois vouloir. Elle me supplie, par
ce moyen, de ne rien entreprendre contre elle. (p.92)

This Svengali-like image later modulates into something more
appealing if no less overwhelming when, according to Breton,
she begins to see him as a god or as the sun (p.130). The oracular
utterances and drawings which are Nadja's precious legacy are
indeed dominated by the theme of submissive love. Breton could
hardly have mistaken the message of emotional dependence in
the following phrases, especially since he transcribes them in
close succession:

Avec la fin de mon souffle, qui est le commencement du
vôtre.
Si vous vouliez, pour vous je ne serais rien, ou qu'une
trace.
Tu es mon maître. Je ne suis qu'un atome qui respire au
coin de tes lèvres ou qui expire. (pp.137-38)

We may speculate that the love-letters which Breton mentions
but does not quote made Nadja's emotional attachment even
more explicit. As for Nadja's drawings, they call on an
unequivocal repertoire of conventional signs of passion —
hearts, arrows, flowers and so forth.

It is interesting to note that Breton tells us that Nadja had
never done any drawing prior to their meeting (p.155): we may
infer that he was the catalyst of this creativity and that, in
broader terms implicating her behaviour at large, he was a
decisive influence on her at this time. It is thus possible that what
Breton was observing was not so much a girl behaving in a
certain way, as a girl behaving in that way *because* she knew
herself to be observed. This would mean that the surrealist
subject may have been the excited witness to magical happenings
of which he was, in fact, the instigator, if not the controller.

One drawing looks to be a self-portrait, Nadja seeing herself
as a sad little girl in a cloak with a huge question-mark inked
round her (p.145). The caption 'Qu'est-elle?' is a poignant echo

of Breton's opening query, and though this document is not discussed in Breton's text, it is made available to the reader as a
clue to Nadja's emotional condition. Specifically, it leads us to
the issue of her psychological disintegration, for Nadja's statements and pictures reflect not only the disturbance of unrequited
passion but also its sequel, mental collapse. Whereas Breton was
observing an exasperating contradiction between mediocrity and
inspiration, Nadja herself was going through a much more painful struggle to reconcile conflicting aspects of herself. At one
level, she was a girl who loved freedom and found it hard to
adapt to any regular demands in life. At another, she was
passionately attracted to a man unable to reciprocate. At a final
level, she found her personality structure too weak to support
these stresses. She began to slip into a schizoid state, responding
to the chaos of her psychic life by losing her grip on reason
altogether.

The symptomatology of Nadja's mental breakdown comes
across with telling sharpness in Breton's account. The evidence
is indisputable. She has auditory and visual hallucinations (two
of her drawings, 'Le Rêve du chat' and 'Le Salut du diable',
being records of the latter: see p.143). She has delusions of
reference, panic fears, deliriums, acute lapses of attention
('absences'). Her conversation drifts away into associative
monologue which Breton may find poetic, but which is none the
less symptomatic of mental instability. One utterance suggests
dissociation between mind and body: speaking of lying in a bath
and feeling her body float away, she says 'Je suis la pensée sur le
bain dans la pièce sans glaces' (p.118). Her drawings are also
consistent with a diagnosis of incipient schizophrenia, for they
contain an abundance of the stylistic features often associated
with the art-works of schizophrenics. These include geometric-
ization; studied insistence on outlines; dislocated parts of the
anatomy; compound images (the doodle on page 147 is a con-
glomerate of some two dozen pictorial signs); and the enigmatic
insertion of isolated letters or words inside the drawing.

Given the wealth of clinical symptoms, it seems incredible that
Breton, a man who likes to notice things, should not have
realized what was really happening to Nadja. He had, after all,

undergone medical training with an orientation towards psycho-pathology, and had actually worked with mental patients. And yet he scarcely makes any mention of Nadja's mental state during the diary of their relationship. The notable exception occurs after Nadja exhibits an unmistakable delirium during which she sees a fiery hand floating over the Seine and even asks Breton 'Tu me crois très malade, n'est-ce pas?' (p.100), an obvious appeal for sympathy. Breton fails to respond, but his next entry contains a lengthy meditation on her condition in which he concedes that 'dans l'état où elle est, elle va forcément avoir besoin de moi' (p.104). Perversely, even here, the 'state' referred to could as well be poverty as mental derangement. It begins to seem that Breton is deliberately evading the issue. Indeed, while it becomes all too clear to the reader that Nadja is losing control, Breton somehow avoids any express mention of madness until as late as page 159, by which time he has told us everything else about her which he ever tells. The final outcome is conveyed in distressingly impersonal terms: 'On est venu, il y a quelques mois, m'apprendre que Nadja était devenue folle' (p.159). Did Breton, the former student of Dr Babinski, have no prior inkling of this? There is a hint of self-disculpation in the coolness of his tone when he goes on to 'explain': 'A la suite d'excentricités auxquelles elle s'était, paraît-il, livrée dans les couloirs de son hôtel, elle avait dû être internée à l'asile de Vaucluse' (pp.159-60). Why 'paraît-il'? Did Breton not trouble to substantiate this information? Did he not, after an intimacy lasting several weeks, feel any urge to visit Nadja in the clinic? We learn nothing more at all about her, so that her later fortunes remain a complete mystery.

The total eclipse of the heroine of the book is clumsily accentuated by a polemical passage which Breton inserts at this point. It consists of an attack on the contemporary psychiatric profession, against which Breton has a pronounced animus. He protests in particular about the unreliability of its diagnostic procedures, the shortcomings of institutional psychotherapy and the arbitrary nature of many internments. Singling out Dr Claude of the Sainte-Anne Hospital, and issuing his photograph as if to say 'Watch out for this man!', Breton accuses him of manipulating patients and callously ignoring their feelings (p.161). Breton adds that if he were ever interned himself, he would at once strangle one of the staff, as a way of getting some peace by being locked up in solitary confinement (pp.166-67)!

As a rehearsal of many ideas which have surfaced in recent years, this lively polemic is a remarkable early document of the 'anti-psychiatry' movement. It is also an important contribution to the corpus of surrealist writings about madness and may be situated in a line of development leading to the campaign to secure the release of Antonin Artaud, that later victim of madness and internment, in 1946. By that very token, the passage sits very ill in its context for the modern reader. If Breton had such strong feelings about incarceration, why did he not take steps to secure Nadja's release? Surely he would tell us if he had? The diatribe only serves to prompt these specific questions. It is as though it were intended to mask a gap in the narrative, only to draw attention to that very gap. We are left with a sense of frustration, and would agree with Michel Beaujour that it has all been 'une aventure bouleversante et ratée' (*23*, p.794).

It does seem curious that a book entitled *Nadja* should shy away from the climax concerning its heroine. Breton seemingly makes a point of telling the full story with documentary precision, and yet, once the adventure falters, he loses interest in dates, glosses over such crucial events as his last visit to Nadja (see p.155), and slides into lacklustre generalizations. The magic has evaporated. Exhilaration gives way to dejection and an air of guilt. The last words of the Nadja section are a fatalistic echo of the anxieties voiced on the book's opening page:

> Qui vive? Est-ce vous, Nadja? Est-il vrai que l'*au-delà*, tout l'au-delà soit dans cette vie? Je ne vous entends pas. Qui vive? Est-ce moi seul? Est-ce moi-même? (p.172)

Winding up the manuscript as far as it had advanced by late August 1927, these lines leave a final impression of isolation and failure. Breton has failed to hold on to Nadja as a lover, and the surrealist vision she refracted for him exists only as a memory.

His last recourse has been to write a text as if, in Roger Navarri's words, to 'réparer les insuffisances du vécu' (*41*, p.192).

And there the text might have rested, woefully suspended on a note of disorientation and doubt, had not Breton been suddenly graced with an encounter that lifted him onto an entirely new plane of enthusiasm and confidence. The postscript he will add in late December 1927 will greatly modify the import of the text abandoned in late August of that year.

Love and beauty

The epilogue to *Nadja* begins with a ponderous account of Breton's dissatisfaction with writing, occasioned by the fatal discrepancy between the artifices of book-making and the confrontation with real-life events. All sense of adventure is now extinguished. The author sees his work as an avowal of failure; he can no longer bear to read the foregoing manuscript; it no longer belongs to him (p.176). The fact that a significant section of the text had seen print that autumn (*1*) may have helped confirm that *Nadja* really was out of its author's hands, a closed book. Moreover, in bidding farewell to his text, Breton seems also to be bidding farewell to Nadja, perhaps even to surrealist adventure generally. The precarious nature of the surrealist enterprise has become all too manifest. Even the Boulevard Bonne-Nouvelle, that elective locale of expectancy, has, after a brief apotheosis at the time of the Sacco-Vanzetti rioting, lapsed into a state of nullity. 'Le boulevard Bonne-Nouvelle, les façades de ses cinémas repeintes, s'est depuis lors immobilisé pour moi comme si la Porte Saint-Denis venait de se fermer' (p.180). The book too has closed like a gate or door, the very opposite of that *porte battante* to which Breton had formerly attributed such virtue (p.18).

That Breton continues to write seems odd: can there be anything to add, since all is said and done? Slowly, by dint of oblique hints, he edges out of depression and opens up to a fresh mood, gradually resurrecting the theme of love. We now gather that in the interim since the composition of the Nadja episode, Breton has met and fallen in love with another woman. She it is who has pointed out to him a new sign to follow, the sky-blue signpost for Les Aubes. (The illustration shows this to be a location near the bridge at Avignon, where, it may be surmised, Breton had gone on a trip with Suzanne Muzard in the latter part of 1927.) Symbolically, a new dawn is being vouchsafed, and the text modulates into a fresh key, slowly elaborating a sequence of luminous and ecstatic images.

The theme of love had, of course, been threaded into the text at all points hitherto. From the outset, the reader had been conditioned to expect Breton's surrealist quest to culminate in an encounter with a beautiful and desirable woman. When Solange bursts on to the stage at the Théâtre des Deux-Masques, she inspires Breton's rapturous observation: 'Une femme adorable entre sans frapper. C'est elle. [...] Brune, châtain, je ne sais. Jeune. Des yeux splendides, où il y a de la langueur, du désespoir, de la finesse, de la cruauté' (pp.48-49). A subsequent discussion of Blanche Derval, who played this role, establishes that Breton is truly magnetized by her beauty, her bold movements, her extraordinary eyes. The prefiguration of the decisive 'entrée en scène' (p.69) of Nadja is obvious. Other women are similarly admired as they pass rapidly yet decisively through Breton's life in what Renée Riese Hubert calls 'an unending flow of flitting analogies' (*32*, p.248), whose common term is the equation of the feminine presence with the surrealist ideal. The last woman in the book, X, marks the consummation of the series. Whereas at an earlier stage Breton touches indefinitely on 'l'événement dont chacun est en droit d'attendre la révélation du sens de sa propre vie' (p.69), and whereas in the company of Nadja he can still speak in evocative yet inconclusive terms of their 'poursuite éperdue' as a 'poursuite de quoi, je ne sais' (p.127), certainty now prevails, and he can speak unhesitatingly about the revelatory climax of the quest. The last few pages of the book swell into a triumphant litany in which X is, phrase by phrase, honoured as the ultimate presence:

Sans le faire exprès, tu t'es substituée aux formes qui m'étaient les plus familières, ainsi qu'à plusieurs figures de mon pressentiment. Nadja était de ces dernières, et il est parfait que tu me l'aies cachée. (p.186)

Breton insists that nothing can henceforth eclipse X's radiance: 'Tu n'es pas une énigme pour moi. Je dis que tu me détournes pour toujours de l'énigme' (p.187). By which, I take it, Breton wants to see X not as an intercessor, a guide to the surreal, but as a literal embodiment thereof, so perfect that further striving becomes unnecessary. The earlier equation of love with clair-voyant powers guiding the lover through the dark labyrinth of experience — the equation underlying Breton's relations with Nadja — is now superseded by a view of love as an illuminating experience wherein shadow and uncertainty can have no place. X is what Robert Champigny calls a 'mythic Idol' (*27*, p.246), and her absolute status implicitly dispels all doubts and resolves all conflicts.

This vision of regenerative love was to be elaborated by Breton in later texts such as *L'Amour fou* and *Arcane XVII* (and finds plentiful echoes in Surrealism at large, for example in the poetry of Eluard or Péret's *Anthologie de l'amour sublime*). It emerges at the end of *Nadja* as a triumphant rebuttal of failure, a grand finale of incandescent confidence. In effect, the presence of X gives Breton the courage to re-evaluate the Nadja episode and to recuperate its ambivalent lessons in terms of a new orientation toward higher things. Whereas the first 'ending' of Nadja had signalled closure, the epilogue opens up the book afresh: '[Tu] es intervenue si opportunément, si violemment et si efficacement auprès de moi sans doute pour me rappeler que je le voulais "battant comme une porte" et que par cette porte je ne verrais sans doute jamais entrer que toi' (p.185).

And yet even now, Breton is not done. Having penned what is in effect an open love-letter to X, he resumes his more sibylline manner and adds yet another postscript. In the space of just over two pages, he imparts a further programmatic dimension to his text with an aesthetic manifesto, a theoretical discourse on convulsive beauty.

Passion is the keynote of this aesthetic theory, Breton insists (p.189). What makes something beautiful for the surrealist poet is its capacity to unite extremes, for instance, the static and the dynamic. Breton expressly rejects the Classical notion of beauty as something frozen, statuesque; equally he refuses the Romantic notion of frenzied beauty, 'plus étourdie qu'un flocon dans la neige' (p.189). The beauty he seeks is one which will reconcile these contraries. The synthesis is given suggestive form in the image of a train trembling on the brink of departure in the Gare de Lyon, at once immobile and on its way. (Breton's 1963 italicization of the word *Lyon* prompts the extra punning association to a lion, i.e. to ferocious strength presumably just held in check.) If this is an image of convulsive beauty, then, says Breton, 'elle est faite de saccades, dont beaucoup n'ont guère d'importance, mais que nous savons destinées à amener une *Saccade*, qui en a' (p.189).

The point here seems to be that beauty, like love, is capable of providing glimpses of a new order which will only be fully instituted once some ultimate 'spasm' has taken place. The phrasing has a declamatory, prophetic ring, but there is little to help the reader pin down *what* is being prophesied. Breton follows this up with a sprinkling of gnomic remarks: about this event being far more important than his personal stake in it; about the human heart as a seismograph; about the sublime virtue of silence. He finally quotes a newspaper cutting about a lost aeroplane. These last-minute riddles hardly clarify the tenor of the prophecy. It is at least clear that convulsive beauty has to do with love, and thus with X; the declaration 'la beauté je la vois comme je t'ai vue' (p.189) makes the equation explicit. But quite what form will be taken by the beauty of the supreme *Saccade* remains unspoken.

I shall shortly suggest that it is possible to discern in these allusions a surrealist programme for social and psychological revolution; but this is only an inference drawn after some reflection, and for the moment I want simply to stress that *Nadja* closes on an intentionally obscure note. Its last sentence — 'La beauté sera CONVULSIVE ou ne sera pas' (p.190) — comes at us with the weight of an imperious parting shot, emphatically capitalized. The proposition cannot really be reduced to an intellectual principle. It is intended passionately, as a kind of rallying cry for the rights of the imagination and the values of

Surrealism. To me, this watchword is Breton's final attempt to propel his reader's attention beyond the text. It is up to us, he seems to be saying, to ensure that surrealist beauty survives, by turning ourselves into people who can react to its spasmodic impact. We must have hearts like seismographs so as to catch the elusive tremors of the surreal. The responsibility for maintaining the surrealist surveillance of reality is thus passed on to the reader in what amounts to a veiled exhortation to apply the risky yet urgent imperatives of Surrealism to his own life.

A surrealist ethos

I want now to develop the suggestion that *Nadja* as a whole represents a kind of allegorical guide to the surrealist way of life. Picking up some of the strands discussed above, I hope to show that they cohere into a pattern equivalent to a tacit code defining authentic surrealist behaviour.

Let us begin by returning to Breton's favourite activity of strolling in the street. Each day, he claims, he spends time patrolling the same section of the Boulevard Bonne-Nouvelle, empty of motive and yet conscious of some kind of impending outcome:

> Je ne sais pourquoi c'est là, en effet, que mes pas me portent, que je me rends presque toujours sans but déterminé, sans rien de décidant que cette donnée obscure, à savoir que c'est là que se passera *cela* (?) (p.38)

It may be noted that the 1928 edition did not italicize that last word, so that Breton must have decided in 1962 to give more impact to his paradox, which is that (a) his sense of what he is likely to encounter is subject to question (i.e. he does not know what to expect), and (b) he senses an identifiable *cela* (i.e. he *does* know what to expect). With a strange faith, Breton is gambling on premonition, engaged in a pursuit of something he cannot define *a priori*.[2] He is thereby postulating a special

___
[2] In the present example, the content of *cela* is not explicit: the 'bonne nouvelle' remains unspoken. We may surmise that when he composed this sentence in

mixture of restlessness and confidence, 'un état d'attente ou de réceptivité parfaite', as he later calls it (*16*, p.141).

The favourite notion of a *quest* arises here. Julien Gracq has offered a whole series of analogues, including voyage of discovery, adventure or crusade, but the notion of the quest is the one which Breton himself preferred. Now, the indispensable precondition for a successful quest carried out by a medieval knight was that he be pure and in a state of grace. Similarly, the precondition for entry into contact with the surreal is an untarnished faith in the validity of one's posture, an ability to 'se mettre en état de grâce avec le hasard, de manière à ce que se passe quelque chose, à ce que survienne quelqu'un' (*15*, p.136). The cycle of events is thus Expectancy — Encounter — Revelation, exactly translating, as Albert Py observes, the surrealist model of automatic writing into terms of real-life action (*65*, p.267). For where the automatist relies on unconscious processes to promote strange and compelling conjunctions of words, full of radiant images, the surrealist walker acquiesces to the flow of the street, relying on chance to provide him with wonderful encounters. The paradox is clear: the surrealist must be at once passive and potentially active. He must be alive to the indiscriminate bustle of signs in the street, while allowing no single thing to channel his attention *until* that moment of the unmistakable signal which focuses all his faculties in an irresistible illumination. The precept of nonchalant vacancy in the first part of the equation is counterbalanced in the second by a brusque mobilization of his total resources.

Elsewhere, Breton manifestly gives value to less demanding sorts of behaviour. He is patently impressed by Nadja's carefree approach to situations, her implementation of 'le comportement lyrique' (*11*, p.77). One day, she takes leave of Breton and walks back to the place where they had met some hours earlier, for no other reason than that this arbitrary choice seems the simplest (p.87). She once went on a nocturnal trip to Fontainebleau with an archeologist to look for ruins in the forest, a search which

early August 1927, Breton had no specific incident in mind and was simply recollecting the pure state of expectancy he had often felt on that stretch of pavement. It is perhaps an example of Objective Chance that what took place a few days later on that very boulevard (albeit in his absence), namely the Sacco-Vanzetti riots of 23 August, was of particular relevance to Breton's project.

common sense might suppose would have been better conducted by daylight (p.133). Her 'irresolute resolution' in such matters charms Breton and inspires him to do likewise. Certainly he likes to present himself as writing in a come-what-may fashion, as I shall show in my next section.

In other instances, Breton commends more flagrant behaviour in which the element of outright scandal is apparent. Wandering the streets at random is one thing; wearing bizarre make-up or styling one's hair to mimic a fairy is quite another! Breton's reaction to Nadja's provocations is positive. It is in the same spirit that he takes the side of the dope-addict and child-murderer Solange in *Les Détraquées*, praising her for her defiant extremism: she and her accomplice are referred to as 'ces superbes bêtes de proie' (pp.55/57). Breton also reminisces proudly about the visits he used to make with Jacques Vaché to the cinemas in Nantes, when they would follow the anti-system of not consulting the programme and, once inside, asking the other spectators what was going on in the film; this would be followed by the outrage of uncorking bottles and eating lunch in the front row — 'à la grande stupéfaction des spectateurs qui n'osaient rien dire' (p.40), adds Breton, somewhat indulgently implying a heroic dimension to what might seem to us more like adolescent rudeness.

Admittedly, there are occasions when Breton's material wears thin. When he tells the anecdote of meeting a girl in the rain who insists on reciting a poem by Rimbaud, we may feel that his admiring comment (with its half-echo of the Rimbaldian *Saison en enfer*) is rather forced: 'C'était si inattendu, si peu de saison' (p.62). Yet we would be missing the point if we isolated the individual example and judged it to be trifling. What matters is the *series* to which it belongs, the constellation of examples which, in combination, bear witness to a strategy for living of far more serious import.

Breton's concern with the question of how to behave in one's daily life has also a wider social and political dimension, reflecting his contemporary preoccupation with left-wing politics. Throughout the twenties, the Russian Revolution remained a heroic example to the French Surrealists, and they spent several years trying to reach a creative understanding with the French Communist Party, which they saw as the only serious revolutionary organization of the time. In a long series of negotiations, in which Breton played a central part, the Surrealist group sought to demonstrate that, as the avant-garde wing of the impending Revolution, it could function within the P.C.F.'s general strategy. However, as it turned out, it was hopeless to suppose that surrealist availability to the demands of chance or the unconscious could ever be reconciled with the discipline of a militant political movement, and these contacts eventually foundered. Breton refers minimally to such matters in *Nadja*, and yet, I would argue, he does sketch out a political credo: one which admits of an *anarchist* rather than a communist reading.[3]

Breton's penchant for Anarchism is specifically disclosed in his reference to the Sacco-Vanzetti riots, which took place in Paris in late August 1927, just as he was coming to the end of his stay at the Manoir d'Ango near Dieppe. The events, as we have seen, occurred on the very boulevard he had so recently designated as the setting of some momentous happening ('c'est là que se passera *cela* (?)'). The riots arose out of protest marches on the day following the news of the execution in America of two working-class anarchists, Nicola Sacco and Bartolomeo Vanzetti, on trumped-up charges. From Breton's exuberant reference to the 'magnifiques journées de pillage dites "Sacco-Vanzetti"' (p.180), it may be inferred that the surrealist, returning to the capital too late to join in, experienced an upsurge of strong emotion and possibly even fantasies about a spontaneous insurrection which had almost come off. Perhaps *this* was the ultimate 'spasm' which Breton wanted to see come about. In the same sentence, he moves on to an obscure avowal of his readiness for insurrection, with this proviso: 'pourvu que le sens le plus absolu de l'amour ou de la révolution soit en jeu et entraîne la négation de tout le reste' (p.180). This is surely enough to alert us to his sympathies: one can readily construe these conditions in anarchist terms as a combination of the

---

[3] For an account of the overt dealings of the surrealist group with Anarchism and Communism, see *64* and *66*.

darker strands of violent anarchism ('négation de tout le reste') with the brighter ones of mutualist anarchism, love and revolutionary idealism merging in a compact which, as a mature surrealist, Breton was to extol so majestically in *Arcane XVII* (wherein, moreover, there occurs an explicit tribute to the Anarchists: *12*, p.14).

Breton's attunement to the anarchist spirit may be further traced to such passages as the polemic against work (pp.78-80), where there are strong echoes of anarchist rhetoric. The diatribe — Breton gives to understand that he voiced it aloud to Nadja at their first meeting, though it is too polished to be anything like a verbatim transcript — makes several robust points, moving from the proposition that routine labour under Capitalism is a hateful and paralysing constraint on man's freedom, to an idealistic evocation of the long yet marvellous progress which can, and eventually will, be made towards throwing off man's social shackles. Before breaking off with a half-apology to the reader ('on voit assez ce que je peux dire à ce sujet'), Breton presents his vision of revolution in terms of the steps taken by a privileged minority whose martyrdom will pave the way for collective emancipation: '[Leurs pas] finiront bien par dessiner une route et sur cette route, qui sait si n'apparaîtra pas le moyen de se désenchaîner ou d'aider à se désenchaîner ceux qui n'ont pu suivre?' (pp.79-80). Such phraseology would seem very much in tune with statements being made at the time about Sacco and Vanzetti.

Given this orientation, it becomes possible to discern in *Nadja* a generalized commendation of gestures of an heroically anarchistic (and sometimes even criminal) type; it is coupled with a forthright condemnation of bourgeois conventions. Breton mentions Gustave Courbet and his part in the demolition of the imperialist Vendôme column during the Paris Commune (p.14). The allusion to Etienne Dolet's statue (p.26) may be explicable in that Dolet was a fighter for intellectual freedom: a radical printer, he was strangled then burned in 1546 for having published blasphemous and seditious works. A reference to the imprisonment of the Marquis de Sade (p.166) may be taken as a reminder of the values which Surrealism associates with that name: aristocratic individualism, allegiance to private desire, willingness to suffer for the avowed singularity of one's nature. Of the women Breton admires, more than one may be said to exhibit an anarchic streak. Fanny Beznos is said to cherish Rimbaud, Nietzsche and Shelley (each in his different way exemplifying a flamboyant and rebellious individualism), and is credited with 'une grande foi révolutionnaire' (p.64). Breton's admiration for the criminal tendencies of the character Solange is accompanied by a hint as to her scorn of social conformities in her choice of dress and her truculent demeanour: 'Mince, très sobrement vêtue, une robe de couleur foncée, des bas de soie noire. Et ce rien de "déclassé" que nous aimons tant' (p.49). At the risk of over-responding to the resonances of *black*, the anarchist colour, one might say that Breton sees in the aberrant black eye-liner used by Nadja an index of her singularity and anarchic daring.

Nadja it is who brings to a head these scattered hints of a political credo nurtured by ill-defined yet potent images of the urban rebel. Her commitment to improvisation and free expression takes on exemplary social import in this context. Her head raised higher than anyone else's in the street (p.72), Nadja is a creature of pride and resource whose allegiance to personal impulse as against orthodox behaviour make of her a prototype of the new woman which, one may surmise, Surrealism was beginning to discover or to invoke. A long passage of praise for her audacious attitude (coming late in the book, it is, sadly, tinged with regret for the brevity of her personal 'rebellion') is cast in the form of somewhat abstract and vague allusions to 'l'émancipation humaine *à tous égards*' (p.168), seemingly a periphrasis for that twinning of social with psychological revolution which Surrealism had by now defined as its goal. It winds up with the suggestion that Nadja is one of those rare beings who become the spontaneous focal point of a kind of libertarian conspiracy: she demonstrates that 'il doit se fomenter autour de chaque être un complot très particulier qui n'existe pas seulement dans son imagination' (pp.168-69). The quintessence of 'lyrical behaviour' is described in the aforementioned foot-note about kissing in the car coming home from Versailles.

Nadja's kiss is most certainly a flagrant act of *amour fou*, and would be admirable for that reason alone. But the footnote stresses yet other virtues, for Breton extrapolates from the single event an extraordinarily dense and lyrical statement about his general perspectives, the most explicit formulation of a surrealist ethos in the whole book.

In Breton's estimation, Nadja qualifies as a member of a class of rare creatures — an élite of the daring and the subversive — who are able to recognize one another by virtue of their 'puissance extrême de défi'. In his memory, the kiss has become a kind of rite of passage, a summons to assume the full dignity of his surrealist vocation. His dearest wish henceforth is to be worthy: 'Idéalement au moins je me retrouve souvent, les yeux bandés, au volant de cette voiture sauvage' (p.179). Finally, Breton extends his fantasy to include a vision of himself not only as the sublime and impetuous lover, but as a bandit with a huge price on his head, who would need to appeal for refuge to his surrealist comrades. Whether in terms of love or crime, the footnote signals the same anarchistic message of solidarity with those marginal beings whose instinct carries them proudly above the petty regulations of society. The episode of the wild kiss becomes a parable of surrealist behaviour at large. Its anarchist connotations merge into the generality of surrealist connotations, in which are subsumed the values of love, defiance, risk, spontaneity, and unconditional faith in a 'principe de subversion totale' (p.179).

Thus it is that *Nadja* articulates an ethos wherein orthodoxy is supplanted by fresh and fluent approaches to thinking and living. The surrealist will obey only the dictates of desire; he will resist capitalist constraints such as work, and subvert the bourgeois ideology of family, patriotism and religion. His vocation impels him to shun stereotyped roles and to confront the problems of existence in a way heedless of social compromise and dismissive of 'le code imbécile du bon sens et des bonnes mœurs' (pp.167-68). Brio and a stylish truculence, instanced in Vaché's mordant wit or Nadja's sublime indifference to common sense, are appropriate touchstones. Scorning the conventional signs which point towards a good job, a good marriage, a good attitude, the surrealist will instead pursue those unconventional signs which point to the possibility of discovering one's personal desires, and, further on, of contributing to man's emancipation at large. Clouded though the text may be by the failure of his relationship with Nadja, Breton does seem to be successful in transmitting a fundamental surrealist doctrine of hope, passion and freedom. It is in this perspective that I am suggesting that his book should be read as, among other things, a persuasive libertarian manifesto.

4. The Authorial Stance

Narrative strategies

If *Nadja* is, in terms of its ethical message, a work of anarchistic rebelliousness, it is equally, at the level of form, a work which sets out to subvert the codes of good literary behaviour. The first unwritten rule which Breton seeks to break is the one which dictates that all creative writing belongs by definition to a larger entity called Literature. To the surrealists, this word meant all that was hateful: comfortable orthodoxy, *belles lettres*, the cultural system at its most smugly reactionary. Their whole strategy, whether as writers of automatic poetry, political pamphlets or any other forms of writing, was to avoid being recuperated by the cultural system and thus ending up as establishment *littérateurs*. This issue was of vital importance to Breton as leader of the movement, and indeed in only the recent past he had broken with Artaud and Soupault because of their supposed 'literary' tendencies.

There are several allusions in *Nadja* to what had by this time become an inescapable tenet of Surrealism. One is Breton's amused reference to the suggestion that Benjamin Péret, automatist, anarchist and violent opponent of Parisian élitism, should have come to the metropolis in order to 'se lancer dans la littérature' (p.33). Another is Breton's emphatic statement towards the end of the book that what matters in life is not that one should write books, but that one should *live* — and above all, live intensely ('la vie *à perdre haleine*', p.173). Finally, there is the moment when real life comes close to eclipsing all thought of writing. When Breton meets X, her presence is so decisive that it makes his book seem redundant: 'Puisque tu existes, comme toi seule sais *exister*, il n'était peut-être pas très nécessaire que ce livre existât' (p.187). One could read this as implying that Breton toyed with the idea of not publishing his manuscript (and even of destroying it).

These anti-literary sentiments are, of course, voiced in a text which, after all, *did* get written, printed and published. Given this concession or compromise, Breton is at pains to stress *within the text* that the work the reader is confronting should not be confused with works of literature, despite superficial resemblances. The second law which Breton proceeds to flout is one of the tacit assumptions of literature, that works normally belong to an identifiable category or genre. How does a writer avoid classification and consequent recuperation? Breton's strategy is to construct his text on a series of incompatible models. *Nadja* becomes a veritable rag-bag of disparate genres. Now it reads like confessional autobiography, now like objective chronicle. It contains superb passages of prose poetry, yet also affects a clinical style of unembroidered 'constatation pure' (p.20). Sometimes it sticks to its point for pages on end; often, it is infuriatingly digressive and whimsical, presenting ideas 'selon le caprice de l'heure qui laisse surnager ce qui surnage' (pp.22/ 24). It indulges in little set-pieces within a host of sub-genres: the reflective essay (e.g. the section paying homage to Nadja as a free spirit, pp.127 ff.); the prose-poem (e.g. the evocation of the Manoir d'Ango, p.69); the tale of the Fantastic (e.g. the 'Bois-Charbons' story, pp.29-30); the dream transcript (pp.57-58); the diatribe (e.g. the polemic against work, pp.78-80); the shaggy-dog story (e.g. the Delouit joke, pp.183-84); the 'whodunit' crime story (e.g. the résumé of *Les Detraquées*, pp.46-53); the moralizing fable (e.g. the tale of the painter in Marseilles, p.175). Parts of the book read like a surrealist version of Freud's *The Psychopathology of Everyday Life*; yet others echo the tradition of the *roman sentimental*. The narrative about Nadja might at times sound like something out of the *Lives of the Saints* or, at other times, like a rather wayward sociological case-study. And on some pages there is a flavour of the fairytale, as if Breton were composing one of those 'contes pour les grandes personnes' of which he speaks in the *Manifeste* (*16*, p.26).

These shifting guises are Breton's way of resisting being pinned down, of avoiding what was perhaps the greatest menace to his intentions — the assimilation of *Nadja* under the heading of Fiction. Indeed his major worry seems to have been that his reader might take his book to be a *novel*, the literary form least compatible with Breton's idea of Surrealism.

In the 1924 *Manifeste*, Breton had singled out the realist novel as the target for his greatest sarcasm. In *Nadja*, he returns to the attack, castigating writers who seek nothing better than to traduce the real in the interest of agreeable artifice. Novels, he argues, distort experience: feigning objectivity, the novelist swaps things around arbitrarily, condensing two people into a single character, changing the colour of a woman's hair, and so on (p.18). Breton seems to feel that novels simply explain things away: they are reductive, even repressive in their denial of the dimensions of feeling and fantasy. But what is really at issue is not so much Breton's distaste for certain decadent forms of Naturalism still current in the twenties, as his desire to produce their opposite — a text which would belong to life rather than to literature, a piece of writing which would assert itself as truth rather than fiction. If we still think in terms of genre, *Nadja* must be placed in a category distinct from all fictions. It purports to be an example, more or less, of the true-life document, as is evident from the insistence with which Breton foregrounds the notion of authenticity.

The most striking feature of the book's format is the photographic illustrations — 44 items in the original, 48 in the revised edition. Of these, about one third are of sites in or near Paris; a further 8 are portraits of real people. Picking up the book, the reader grasps very quickly that this is not a *photo-roman* but a work of strict documentation. Through these pictures, the author can bring what he has to say into immediate focus. Thus we read that Nadja and Breton are sitting outside a wineshop in the Place Dauphine: at once this setting appears before our eyes (p.86). We read of Péret's arrival in Paris, and there he is, grinning happily at us from the page opposite (p.32). Paintings by De Chirico and Braque, a cinema leaflet, a two-page letter addressed to Breton, Nadja's drawings — all these are genuine first-hand documents; it is as if Breton were saying, 'If you don't believe what I say, then I will show you'.

This visual documentation is generally convincing and

certainly at odds with our normal literary experience. Whereas in a work of fiction we are asked to imagine how people look, here we actually see them. Settings are presented with equal directness and plausibility: the appearance of the Porte Saint-Denis or the Château de Saint-Germain can be verified by anyone who takes the trouble to go there. Admittedly there are some unverifiable items, victims of the passage of time: Dolet's statue is now gone, the Hôtel des Grands Hommes has closed, and one will seek in vain today the Sphinx Hotel on the Avenue Magenta. Yet because enough of the photographs are authentic, the reader will tend to take the rest on trust.

Further gestures of authentication are provided within Breton's text. He cites some fifty proper names of actual people in the course of the book. He gives precise dates, as when he mentions first meeting Nadja, a little after office closing-time, on 4 October, with a footnote (itself scrupulously dated 1962!) to specify the year as 1926. He makes a point of giving addresses: Nadja lives at the Hôtel du Théâtre, Rue de Chéroy. The eccentric woman she meets one night leaves a visiting card which is duly transcribed: 'Madame Aubry-Abrivard, femme de lettres, 20, rue de Varenne, 3e étage, porte à droite' (p.120). Such pedantry conduces to a sense of authenticity and completeness which tends to validate the preposterous or the unimaginable as being of a piece with the acceptable, the only-too-real. Each instance of the marvellous seems to be balanced by a verified fact.

A further aspect of the book confirms our sense of contact with the real world. It is the 'open' nature of the text. Unlike most literary fictions, which are autonomous and integrated compositions, *Nadja* lacks integration, and is certainly far from being autonomous, since it beckons unto itself whole flurries of extraneous documents and data. Circling in implied orbits around the book are the history of Surrealism in the twenties, the biographies of Breton and his contemporaries, the actual books, pictures and objects to which he refers. The enthusiastic researcher is given dozens of leads to follow. He can, for instance, track down the text of *Les Détraquées*, published in 1956 in a surrealist magazine, or of De Chirico's fantastic novel

Hebdomeros, which Breton recommends (p.15). I have amused myself with researches of an extra-literary kind, verifying the tangible existence of the bronze glove and certain of Nadja's drawings, and visiting locations mentioned in *Nadja*. Within the field of criticism, the book has equally remained open to discussion, stimulating dozens of articles and chapters in books. The present study is an addition to a dossier which seems unlikely to be closed for some while yet.

Within this context of fidelity to historical fact, one crucial mode of writing remains to be discussed, that of the day-to-day journal. The central two-fifths of the text dealing with Nadja is divided into dated entries covering the period 4 to 12 October 1926, and is couched in the typical diary-keeper's tense, the present. The entries bear signs of stylization, and indeed the diary proper is framed by discursive prose in the past tense, suggesting that the shift into the present is a conscious device. Yet this manner of immediacy, and the evident concern for detail — Breton must surely have kept some sort of notebook during this period — are sufficient to bring the reader into a close sense of participation. Diaries are normally addressed to no specific reader other than their author: to be party to an unguarded and seemingly guileless statement of facts is to be inclined to believe them. To read someone's diary is to re-experience the actuality of part of someone's real life, a consciousness responding directly, day by day. The impression of an undoctored logging of unpredictable events adds a further impetus to the textual thrust away from literary contrivance. 'Tu écriras un roman sur moi. [...] De nous il faut que quelque chose reste' is Nadja's encouragement to Breton (p.117). Ironically, the uncultured girl assumes that an account of their affair must be cast in the form of a novel. But Breton, to ensure that 'something remains' of their relationship, deliberately adopts a more convincing mode.

The Nadja diary may be seen as a structural paradigm of the book at large. It is discontinuous, full of haphazard and unexplained transitions. It reflects real life, as shapeless as free association. Above all, it develops across a long period. *Nadja* as a whole resembles a diary in that it tends to foreground the dates and circumstances of its own construction as it goes along, so that to read it is to follow an evolution through a punctuated temporal span. Let us consider the sequence of extra-textual events which govern the accumulation of the various component parts across time.

The sequence is as follows. In October 1926, Breton meets Nadja and may be assumed to start a diary, the outline for the central section of the book. By late 1926 he has lost touch with her, learning of her internment in a mental hospital in early 1927 (see p.159). While staying at the Manoir d'Ango in August 1927, Breton composes most of the book, recapitulating events dating back over the previous decade of his life; he interrupts this work at the end of the month (p.176). The equivalent of pages 9-172 in the Folio edition would have been written by this point. Did Breton feel his project was complete? He is happy to publish a lengthy extract from his manuscript in the review *Commerce* in autumn 1927 (*1*). During the interval, he has begun collecting documents to illustrate the intended book version, engaging his fellow surrealist Jacques Boiffard to take special photos. But other things are happening in his life: above all he meets and falls in love with Suzanne Muzard. When he scans the manuscript and decides to take up his pen to write an epilogue, in which he addresses his new mistress simply as 'X', it is already late December 1927: the text closes on a press-cutting dated 26 December (p.190). A further extract from the *Nadja* diary having appeared in print in March 1928 (*2*), the completed book, with illustrations, is at last published in May 1928 (*3*). But again it is worth remembering that Breton cannot resist further work on *Nadja* when, in late 1962, he modifies it in considerable detail, and adds new photos plus a preface, dated Christmas 1962 and ironically titled 'dépêche retardée' (*6*).

All these dates can be inferred from the text itself or from simple bibliographical research. What emerges is a picture of spasmodic development in which the book as we have it advanced only with difficulty into its final form — in one sense, it took Breton thirty-five years to get it right! The most significant gap in composition, between August and December 1927, corresponds to that period in Breton's private life when he shifted from the despondency occasioned by the Nadja episode to the euphoria of a new relationship. In the Folio version, this interval is signalled by a simple gap on the page, whereas the original 1928 edition had a whole blank leaf at this point (*3*, pp.193-94). The notion of a gap or shift in viewpoint is important: the interval in the text is also the place where real life flows into the narrative, a further demonstration of the book's porousness to extra-literary experience.

In these various ways, *Nadja* is offered to the reader as a document which proclaims its own authenticity. Breton explicitly claims to be sincere, to expose his life to others, to inhabit what he calls a house of glass in which the virtues of transparency and frankness act as guarantees of ultimate integrity. 'Pour moi, je continuerai à habiter ma maison de verre [...] où je repose la nuit sur un lit de verre aux draps de verre, où *qui je suis* m'apparaîtra tôt ou tard gravé au diamant' (pp.18-19). The ambition thus expressed is reminiscent of that passion for total exposure and hence total honour manifested by Michel Leiris in *L'Age d'homme*, where Leiris speaks of his own auto-biographical practice as being to 'rejeter toute affabulation et n'admettre pour matériaux que des faits véridiques [...], rien que ces faits et tous ces faits' (*60*, p.14). Leiris goes on to refer to *Nadja* as a model in this enterprise of scrupulous avowal. He points up the dangers of such self-revelation in the image of the bullfighter squaring up to the bull — a situation where honour tends to be synonymous with vulnerability. In Breton's case, there does emerge an instinctive equation between the act of writing and the impulse to adopt a vulnerable stance. He has made it clear that the automatic experiments of *Les Champs magnétiques* early in his career were in many ways a hazardous adventure with no known co-ordinates; others of his books also make disclosures which place Breton in an exposed position. In the case of *Nadja*, the implicit confession of his failure to help a distressed girl makes the book potentially embarrassing and even painful for him. But I feel that it is characteristic of Breton's whole policy as a writer that he should systematically expose himself, and in this sense shift the reader's focus from evaluation of the text as literature to evaluation of its author as a man.

Omissions and ambiguities

'Je persiste à réclamer les noms, à ne m'intéresser qu'aux livres qu'on laisse battants comme des portes, et desquels on n'a pas à chercher la clef' (p.18). Breton's stand at the outset of *Nadja* is one of unflinching dedication to candour. Later, in *L'Amour fou*, he will expatiate on this principle, insisting on the need for unstinting accuracy and exhaustiveness in the documentation of surrealist experience. 'Pas un incident ne peut être omis, pas même un nom ne peut être modifié sans que rentre aussitôt l'arbitraire. La mise en évidence de l'irrationalité immédiate, confondante, de certains événements nécessite la stricte authenticité du document humain qui les enregistre' (*11*, p.59).

Such rhetoric encourages the view that *Nadja* is a work of faithful reportage in all respects. When Breton ridicules novelists who alter the colour of a real woman's hair, we can only assume that his allusions to the colour of Nadja's hair — 'une blonde', 'ses cheveux d'avoine' (pp.72 and 83) — are unimpeachably accurate. In an enthusiastic moment, one critic, Maurice Nadeau, exclaims: 'rien d'imaginé dans *Nadja*, tout est parfaitement, rigoureusement vrai' (*63*, p.166). But should we be so ready to take Breton's word for it? If we turn up the photo of Nadja on page 129 we will find the tone of the reproduction too dark for any positive confirmation of blondness. Might not Breton have adjusted this detail?

A minimum of doubt can be enough to send us back for a more critical inspection of Breton's claims. On second thoughts, we may wonder whether his chosen modes of exposition — the documentary report, the sober photographs, the dated diary — are not just as capable as more overtly 'literary' modes of throwing up a smoke-screen and effecting what Michel Bertrand and Roger Navarri have both called 'une mise en condition du lecteur' (*24*, p.85 and *41*, p.187).

It would be naïve, of course, to demand that Breton detail

every single aspect of, say, his relationship with Nadja. Breton concedes that he is predominantly interested in 'les épisodes les plus marquants de ma vie' (p.19), and has made it plain in other contexts that his 'moments nuls' (*16*, p.17) are not what he would choose to commemorate in print. That Breton does not 'tell all' is, in this superficial sense, perfectly acceptable. After all, what he had for tea on 4 October 1926 is of no moment.

Even so, the alert reader, while keeping matters in due proportion, will surely want to examine certain facts more closely. Robert Champigny points out that, of course, it would be silly to try to authenticate the colour of Madame Bovary's hair, since that colour is *by definition* identical to what Flaubert says it is: 'In fiction, all that can be checked is the wording' (*27*, p.243). But once we are unequivocally informed that Nadja was a real-life person, then the span of reference at once opens up to that of Paris in the late twenties, and we are entitled to seek such verifications as we see fit. If literal truth is foregrounded as a value in the text, we have every right to go looking for it.

Now, as a dossier, *Nadja* is not nearly as complete as we might at first suppose. In the epilogue, Breton acknowledges several omissions beyond his control. It was impossible to obtain a photo of the statue of Henry Becque, which had been hidden by palings; he had been refused permission to photograph in the Musée Grevin (pp.177/79). This seems fair enough: he did at least try. (And indeed the revised edition of 1963 makes amends by printing new photos of just these two items.) But what of the documents which Breton cites yet fails to reproduce? There is explicit reference to a manuscript by De Chirico — 'un cahier manuscrit que j'ai entre les mains' (p.14) — of which no further detail is released. What of Nadja's letters? None of these is publicly reproduced apart from a fragment dated 15 November 1926 which appeared on the jacket of the 1964 Livre de Poche edition (*7*), only to be discarded by the publishers of the 1972 Folio paperback (*8*). Breton does reveal ten of Nadja's drawings, but at least as many more remain unseen, including, for example, the self-portrait he describes in which Nadja's body takes the form of a light-bulb fitted with butterfly wings (p.155).

To some extent these material omissions may be justifiable in terms of the difficulties of finding appropriate photos, or of reproducing faintly pencilled material, as Breton hints (p.143); there may even have been copyright problems, as in the case of the De Chirico manuscript. But it is not always possible to give Breton the benefit of the doubt as regards his text. At times, he seems quite deliberately to avoid telling all. On one occasion, Nadja is praised for having made an uncannily accurate guess as to the substance of an explanatory text which Max Ernst had stuck on the back of his playfully titled canvas *Les Hommes n'en sauront rien* (p.149). But although Breton reproduces the picture, he fails to quote either Ernst's text, or what Nadja actually said; we have only Breton's word for it that there was any sort of uncanniness about the incident at all. Such withholding of evidence beins to look like wilful evasion; the reader wonders whether he is not being hoodwinked.

Mystification through omission is perhaps an inappropriate charge to level at a self-declared work of caprice. All the same, is it not odd that a writer so keen to provide a thorough picture of his situation should relay so little information about the generality of his existence? We can only assume that Breton regularly attended the surrealist café during the period in question. Or was he conspicuously absent in October 1926? What political activities was he pursuing? What sort of life was he leading in material terms? Did he really have all the time in the world to spend on Nadja — and the money? Further, given that love is such an insistent Bretonian theme, he seems strangely reticent about his relations with actual women. In *Nadja*, his wife Simone is scarcely mentioned. What did *she* think about Nadja? (From other sources we know that Breton divorced Simone a couple of years later.) Nadja herself is presented over a period as a reliable living presence — but only over a period. Her disappearance into the Vaucluse asylum is an event dismissed in a phrase — and, once she has gone, all we have left is a photograph so doctored as to be useless, and a name which, we suddenly remember, is not even her real name. It is as though, once she passes beyond physical reach, Breton immediately bans further material revelations, the better to facilitate her accession to the plane of myth.[4]

[4] A curious article by Marcel Mariën (*37*) alleges that Nadja was none other than

The person whom Breton most blatantly mythifies is the woman encountered at the climax of the book. 'Je persiste à réclamer les noms', writes Breton in August 1927. Yet, addressing his new mistress in the epilogue composed four months later, he has already forgotten his own stipulation, calling her simply 'tu' and censoring all mention of her name (as he later states, 'pour ne pas la désobliger'; *20*, p.90). Only in the course of a surrealist enquiry about love in *La Révolution surréaliste* in December 1929 did Breton spell out her real name, Suzanne Muzard (and, to my knowledge, in no other public text of his). This anonymity strikes a discordant note in a book which began with such emphatic claims to frankness. It marks the shift from authentic diary-time to a kind of timelessness in which the beloved is transfigured into the nameless Eternal Feminine. For the reader who has been led to believe that a final 'revelation' will accrue after he has tackled all the mysteries of the book, this secrecy *in extremis*, this clouding of the final message, can have an alienating effect. As Pierre Testud complains: 'A la chronique minutieuse des rencontres avec Nadja s'est substituée l'incarnation amoureuse, dont le caractère intime en même temps qu'essentiellement allusif donne au lecteur le sentiment d'être exclu de l'œuvre' (*46*, p.581).

These dissatisfactions about Breton's authorial stance are further reflected at the level of his actual style of writing. Certain aberrations become acutely manifest in the light of assertions made in Breton's 1962 preface. Here Breton makes the trenchant and, at first sight, plausible claim that he had intended the account of his experiences to be cool and scientific. Invoking his anti-literary principles, he alludes to the strategy of substituting illustrations for inane description and then claims that 'le ton adopté pour le récit se calque sur celui de l'observation médicale, entre toutes neuropsychiatrique, qui tend à garder trace de tout ce qu'examen et interrogatoire

Blanche Derval, a woman eleven years Breton's elder: the cover-up was for reasons of propriety and embarrassment. Mariën's article is itself impeccably documented, down to an extract from the Brussels telephone directory listing Derval's name, her death certificate dated 24 August 1973, and a photo of her gravestone. Unfortunately the actual link between Blanche and Nadja seems unproven except by hearsay. I therefore prefer to set aside this hypothesis — along with the preposterous one voiced by Roger Shattuck, that Nadja was murdered by persons unknown (see *44*, p.55).

peuvent livrer, sans s'embarrasser en le rapportant du moindre apprêt quant au style' (p.6).

Breton presumably has in mind medical reports such as he would have encountered during his youthful employment as a psychiatric orderly. The case-history devoid of stylistic embellishment may indeed be a good model for a documentary work of this kind, and yet Breton's claim to have compiled something like a scientific report can hardly be seen as more than a pious wish, despite what some early critics seem to have thought. The text of Breton's 1922 piece 'L'Esprit nouveau' might be said to be uniformly bald and colourless, but not, I would contend, that of *Nadja* — despite Michel Carrouges's praise of the 'austère coloration du récit, magnifiquement grise' (*57*, p.221). Far from being grey and uniform, Breton's narrative is in fact alive with emotive shades of poetic colour. It has a style of persuasive brilliance rather than of scientific neutrality; it is designed not to inform, but to seduce.

Aspects of Breton's style have been analysed by such critics as Bertrand, Bürger, Champigny, Navarri and Prince (see *24*, *25*, *27*, *41* and *42*). All agree that, taken overall, the text of *Nadja* is far more complex and troubled than Breton would have us believe. In contrast to the psychiatrist taking clinical notes, Breton is not at all inclined to suppress feeling. He is, rather, passionately involved in what he is saying, and where he does step back from events, it is not in a spirit of cool reflection, but in a mood of marvelling. Often his style is hyperbolic and lyrical, full of those keywords typical of Surrealism: *vertige*, *caprice*, *invraisemblable*, *singulier*, *merveille* and so forth. The authorial voice is hardly noticeable for its self-restraint. As Champigny has suggested (*27*, pp.243-44), many Bretonian sentences are launched with a stock phrase borrowed from the oratory of lawyers or preachers: 'Je dois avouer que...', 'C'est à partir de telles réflexions que...', 'En ce qui me concerne...', 'Je m'assure que...' (examples from pages 9-18). The effect of such formulae is to institute an elevated, self-important tone, entirely at odds with the notion of an intimate confession. Breton's recourse to extended anaphora is similarly an index of his mannered self-awareness as he presses rhythmically and purposefully towards more and more lofty meanings. Thus the address to X fashions a litany of adoration out of the nine-fold repetition of the nominative phrase 'Toi qui...' (including the variants 'Toi que...' and 'Toi' plus complement: see pp.185-86). In another reverential passage in praise of Nantes, Breton sustains a sentence of fifteen lines in which the town-name punctuates a crescendo of mounting fervour, a repeated magic word invoking a mystical force beyond analysis (pp.33/35).

The ornateness of Breton's lengthier sentences can sometimes degenerate into a rhetoric of empty flourishes and what Champigny calls 'gestures of circumscription' (*27*, p.244) where the bare bones of a proposition are wrapped in elegant but unnecessary periphrasis. Such features suggest a rather mannered hand at work, especially since in the 'Avant-dire' Breton admits to being motivated by 'quelque égard au mieux-dire' (p.7), a formulation which itself reeks of preciosity. The fact remains that, of all Breton's books, this was the only one he saw fit to revise. Quite apart from modifications of content or layout, there are dozens of passages where he could not resist making the most pernickety alterations. The fullest account of these emendations is given by Claude Martin (*38*), though even he foregoes the listing of the hundreds of substituted nouns, inserted commas, re-ordered clauses and so forth. 'Il n'est peut-être pas interdit de vouloir obtenir un peu plus d'adéquation dans les termes et de fluidité par ailleurs' (p.6), is Breton's justi-fication. And yet, is there an obligation for us to see such retouching as an innocent procedure? It is surely symptomatic of a relationship to the text which is uneasy and undignified. Breton may have been justified in adjusting the occasional solecism or in inserting what, on later reflection, was a more telling epithet. Yet one cannot help feeling that his nursing of a text which had been in circulation for decades is both highly dubious in a surrealist and disagreeably suggestive of a lingering sense of culpability and incompleteness. Breton, three decades later, cannot leave well alone.

Over and above the explicit discussion of style in the 'Avant-dire', Breton's book repeatedly foregrounds the issue of its own manner. Many sentences embody their own self-reflexive commentary, the text signalling itself as code as well as message. Gerald Prince has argued that such 'meta-narrative signs' are a profuse and insistent feature of the book (he has counted over a hundred instances; see *42*, pp.343-44). They form a gloss on the discourse which forces the reader to attend on two levels — on the one hand, there is something happening (the 'story'); on the other, there is the writing which is itself 'happening' (the text). And there are times when Breton's first-person singular seems less intent on furnishing perspectives on experiences from life than on stage-managing a series of linguistic events, a thrilling spectacle of verbal *tours de force*.

On reflection, we may want to see the book's opening remarks on the principles of its own composition in a new light. Those effusive announcements about caprice and improvisation may begin to sound exhibitionistic, suggesting a 'deliberate capriciousness' which equates to a stylistic stratagem rather than genuine artlessness. It seems indeed the intention that the reader should be hooked on the promise of freedom, the happy-go-lucky mood of the 'caprice de l'heure qui laisse surnager ce qui surnage' (p.24). We may surmise that it is not always Breton's unconscious mind, with its impromptu inventions and slapdash transitions, which is in the ascendant, but the authorial 'I', the wide-awake exponent of a central stylistic authority.

This is to posit a degree of self-conscious posing in the authorial stance of groping in the dark. Each time we notice what Navarri calls the 'côté tâtonnant de la phrase' (*41*, p.189), we may want to say that this fumbling is as much a stylistic ploy as the reflection of a genuine uncertainty. I have argued earlier that there might be something fishy going on in Breton's omissions, which he dismisses as the result of some 'oubli sincère' (p.24). Now it is that one wants to analyse that very disclaimer, and contest its honesty. How can an authentic lapse of memory be motivated by sincerity? One may sincerely regret, one may sincerely desire, but surely not *sincerely forget*!

Marc Bertrand has spoken of a 'pratique rigoureuse de l'indétermination' (*24*, p.85), and has persuasively analysed the ways in which Breton's text transmits a paradoxical knowledge-cum-ignorance. And Peter Bürger comments that, in Breton, extreme syntactical precision tends to accompany extreme semantic imprecision, such that definition is always indefinitely deferred. This 'language in which exactitude repeatedly modulates into imprecision' (*25*, p.129) is an elaborately staged performance in which a veil is constantly on the point of being lifted; and on the rare occasions when the veil *is* lifted, another veil comes into sight.

I shall round off this brief register of Breton's shortcomings with two last specimens of evasive writing. They are sentences occurring during the highly charged description of Nadja as she approaches Breton on the Rue Lafayette. Almost the first remark describing his impressions is: 'Un sourire imperceptible erre peut-être sur son visage' (p.72). Now, the basic proposition is clear: there is a smile on a woman's face. But this proposition is three times qualified in such a way as to undermine its positiveness. Firstly, the smile is said to be imperceptible: logically, it thereby becomes impossible that it should be perceived at all, and a smile which cannot be perceived is hardly a smile! Secondly, the smile is imprecisely located. If we normally expect the cliché of a smile playing on someone's lips, then the statement that it is 'wandering around' on someone's face is rather pointedly vague. Finally, there is the disclaimer *peut-être*, which throws the whole statement into a further reach of doubt. All in all, we may conclude that there *was* no actual smile on Nadja's face — or that it exists only in the imagination of the witness, or again in the words of the writer. It begins to look as though the language is coaxing the reader to give credence to a perception as fact at the same time as the protagonist-reporter is busy relinquishing all responsibility for that fact.

Nadja's *entrée en scène* is thus shrouded in imprecision, drawn out by the subsequent evocation of her fanciful make-up. Only after some while does Breton proceed with the narrative, stepping up to Nadja without hesitation, as if assuming control of the situation. Now it is that a true smile appears on Nadja's face, a distinct and perceptible response. And yet Breton will write of it: 'Elle sourit, mais très mystérieusement, et, dirai-je, comme *en connaissance de cause*, bien qu'alors je n'en puisse rien croire' (p.73). Breton's penchant for ambiguity is once more in evidence. He definitely sees Nadja smile, definitely registers a perceptual fact — but at once seeks to render that fact less crisp and incisive by the gloss 'très mystérieusement'. This swaying between certainty and uncertainty is repeated when Breton firstly attributes to Nadja an air of confident recognition (*'en connaissance de cause'*), then disqualifies this attribution by pleading disbelief ('je n'en puisse rien croire'). What *exactly* is he saying? Did Nadja's smile convey a sense of complicity, or did it not? We shall never know, and must content ourselves with the text as it stands. As with a work of fiction, all that can be checked is the wording.

Such equivocation on the author's part, discernible at the micro-textual level of such sentences as these as well as the macro-textual level at which is posed the whole issue of the plausibility of surrealist experience, leaves an awkward impression. I do find it embarrassing that Breton should so airily sidestep his own stipulations, carrying out unjustified acts of ellipsis and occultation. I am not happy to observe stylistic mannerisms which detract from the impression of naturalness, making the text seem more coquettish than capricious. There do seem to be passages where the book edges towards artifice and away from authenticity, thereby becoming a work of literary effect instead of that document conditioned by real life which had been promised. The reader sensitive to such aspects of the text may well feel an obscure sense of disappointment.

5. Conclusion

What kind of a book is *Nadja*? In sketching some answers to this question, I have hoped at least to show that we are dealing with a uniquely provocative text which needs to be approached with respect for its many challenges. Breton has, I believe, blazed a trail that is still warm, and any commentary on that trail in cold print can be no more than an exposition of, rather than a definitive solution to, the problems it raises. My closing remarks are therefore simply a summary of my principal suggestions, with a pointer to what I see as the lesson to be drawn from the reading experience.

On the one hand, we have seen how Breton flouts literary convention by writing to the rule of caprice and implementing such a flurry of conflicting literary models that the text never seems to come to rest. On the other hand, I have argued that there are identifiable patterns of preoccupation within the work, sufficient to justify analysis along traditional thematic lines. We can be assured that Breton is indeed dealing with the disposition of clues to the surreal, and that, true to its title, the book nominates Nadja as the medium of this new order. Drawing largely on her example, Breton also sketches a code of behaviour — anti-authoritarian and improvisatory — which the reader is tacitly encouraged to adopt for himself. All in all, a reasonably cogent ideology can be disengaged from the shifting surface of the text.

Having said this, I must still acknowledge that, in many respects, *Nadja* remains puzzling and inconclusive. At times, Breton betrays bourgeois reflexes, unwarranted waverings and reticences. Often his relish of the 'faits de valeur intrinsèque sans doute peu contrôlable' (p.20) leads him disastrously to foreground the trivial. His semantic and stylistic investment in 'Enigmatics' sometimes looks like shabby mystification; above all, his policy of keeping the reader in the dark about key details concerning Nadja and X may suggest a suspect inclination to secrecy. Further still, some passages may be said to evince an excessive concern for deliberate rhetorical effects, and thus to constitute manipulative 'literature' rather than neutral 'document'.

Of course each reader must assess the relative weight of these charges before making his personal evaluation. My own view is that it would be hard to defend Breton as being unimpeachably consistent and candid. And yet it would equally be unfair to insist that he is an unreliable trickster. Far from it. On many counts, Breton's failings may be forgiven, if not forgotten. After all, unless the reader is a stubborn 'amateur de solutions faciles' (p.96), he ought to concede that the *faits-glissades* and the *faits-précipices* are *of their essence* paradoxical and unfathomable. Further, Breton's authority over his medium is itself only relative. He may seduce his reader by exploiting certain techniques (and this is, after all, only what any worth-while writer must do); but he is also *himself* a reader who queries his own text, just as doubtful about whether it is making sense, whether it will lead him from bewilderment to insight.

I feel it of paramount importance to relate these issues to a fundamental crisis of ambition which, I would suggest, beset Breton once he began to write in July 1927. Seemingly he had no fixed idea as to where his text ought to head, except that it must at some stage coincide with the trajectory of Nadja. The strategy and tone of the writing can scarcely be disentangled from Breton's emotional state. He had met a woman who had shown him the path to a new life, and yet he had abandoned her and strayed from that path. His retrospective appreciation of that glimpsed direction became problematic in that its very nature was to lead away from orthodox understanding. Breton was himself still struggling to break out from conventions of thought and behaviour. Moreover, he urgently wanted to engage with values which would transcend the merely literary. How then write a book which would break the bookish mould? How be a writer and also a man loyal to 'la vie à *perdre haleine*'?

Breton's ideological orientation obliged him to give priority to real-life encounters over fictional ones. And yet, in the writing, the narrative of his affair with Nadja inevitably turned out to be something sad and curtailed, a 'story', an inadequate substitute for the real thing which had slipped from his grasp. A crisis of a moral and existential kind, arising out of his hesitancies regarding a woman to whom he was attracted but whose madness scared him, shades imperceptibly into the crisis of Breton's relationship to writing itself.

Maybe the text as completed in August 1927 fell short of Breton's ambitions; maybe no book could be expected to delineate the surreal in a convincing way. Yet, at the last, Breton was able to shake off his lethargy and to take a decision. Rather than suppress a text in which, in many respects, he cuts an equivocal and occasionally sorry figure, he had the courage to publish it, and so to expose his shortcomings. To some extent he thereby resolved the problem of the gap between writing and living. 'La vie est autre que ce qu'on écrit' (p.82). Yet the publication of one's confession is an act within life as well as, inevitably, a contribution to literature.

From this debate about motives and relationships, the reader is free to infer a number of things about Breton in particular and Surrealism at large. He may adopt an attitude of censure or approval, relating the content of the book to the ambitions sketched in its preface, and passing judgment on its impact and its authenticity. But I feel that, if he is at all responsive, he will attend to the underlying system of values which, in my opinion, is the mainstay of the book. Breton may well fall short of his own formulated standards — this is his human failing. And yet his work can outlive his personal frailty and be a manifesto of surrealist ideals still worth pursuing. Values such as expectancy, availability, love, convulsive beauty, freedom and rebellion remain for us to ponder and prize.

Perhaps the greatest achievement of *Nadja* as a text is that it shapes the reader in new ways, and encourages him to alter his habits. Perplexed at first, he is gradually coaxed into an attitude of receptivity, learning that, just like life, *Nadja* needs to be deciphered like a cryptogram and that this deciphering requires the marshalling of novel resources. Reading this book carefully means tuning into the resonances of signs linked by poetic analogy. What I have termed serial perception is that practice of scanning in which the mind is alert to resemblances, receptive to the metaphoric correspondences which are like lights flashing across the darker reaches of the book. Michel Beaujour likens *Nadja* to a deck of cards which we are entitled to deal out in whatever patterns we choose (*23*, pp.781-82). Now it would be wrong to say that the meaning of the book is entirely aleatory, since the nature of this pack is to conduce to certain elective groupings. None the less, Beaujour's allusion to the reader's participation is entirely apposite. That 'intensification through analogies' of which Renée Riese Hubert speaks (*32*, p.249) is directly dependent on the emergence of an affinity or reciprocity between writer and reader. The full potency of the text is released only when they share in the process of serial discovery and begin together to shape a continuity out of the swirling circumstances of the narrative. If Breton could claim that he and Nadja were the object of powers associated with some nameless finality — 'objet que nous nous voyions de démarches ultimes, d'attentions singulières, spéciales' (pp.128/30) — so writer and reader may equally entertain the notion of a collaboration governed by pressures external to their conscious control, and edging towards a revelation of unsuspected concord.

Some will say there is a case for seeing *Nadja* as a frustrating failure. But perhaps there is an exactly congruent case for seeing it as that sort of flawed work which pivots into success by virtue of its tragic tensions and its persistence in emitting signals which cross both time and the gap between reading and living. If the reader of *Nadja* can accept the authority of 'le cœur humain, beau comme un sismographe' (p.190), there is hope that the outcome of his various textual encounters will be an emotional impetus carrying him further than intellectual analysis, in the direction of that dangerous yet paramount project of restoring poetic values to life. 'Qu'on se donne seulement la peine de *pratiquer* la poésie', Breton once exclaimed (*16*, p.28). The reader loyal to the spirit of *Nadja* could adopt no better motto.

Bibliography

This bibliography lists the most significant material specific to the study of *Nadja*, and includes a selection of more general publications which contain discussions of that work.

Where no place of publication is given, the place is Paris.

I. FRENCH EDITIONS OF 'NADJA'

1. '*Nadja*. Première partie', *Commerce*, 13 (automne 1927), 77-120. Opening section of Breton's text, corresponding to pp.9-69 in *8*.
2. '*Nadja* (fragment)', *La Révolution surréaliste*, 11 (15 mars 1928), 9-11. Extract from the diary section dated 6 October, corresponding to pp.87-103 in *8*. With illustration of painting by De Chirico.
3. *Nadja*, Gallimard, Collection Blanche, 1928 (25 mai). (Dépôt légal 28 juillet 1928.) 219 pages. With 44 numbered illustrations and corresponding 'Table des gravures'. Pages 75-76 and 193-94 are blank. This first edition of *Nadja* in book form was issued with the publicity slogan 'Pour les femmes de 25 à 30 ans — pour une femme de 25 à 30 ans'.
4. *Nadja*, Gallimard, 1945. Re-issue of *3*.
5. *Nadja*, Gallimard, 1949. Re-issue of *3*.
6. *Nadja*. *Edition entièrement revue par l'auteur*, Gallimard, Collection Blanche, 1963. 161 pages. With 48 un-numbered illustrations, including modifications or additions to the original 1928 selection. Contains textual revisions throughout, including the addition of a preface, entitled 'Avant-dire (dépêche retardée)' and dated Christmas 1962. This constitutes the definitive text.
7. *Nadja*, Gallimard, Livre de Poche No. 1233, 1964. 187 pages. 48 illustrations. Text as *6*. With jacket illustrations, including the partial reproduction of an unpublished letter from Nadja to Breton dated 15 November 1926.
8. *Nadja*, Gallimard, Collection Folio No. 73, 1972. 190 pages. 48 illustrations. Text as *6*. With single jacket illustration. This is the edition to which reference is made in this study.

II. ENGLISH TRANSLATIONS OF 'NADJA'

9. '*Nadja* (Opening chapter)', tr. Eugene Jolas, *transition*, 12 (March 1928), 28-50.
10. *Nadja*, tr. Richard Howard, New York: Grove Press/London: Evergreen Books, 1960, 160 pp. 44 illustrations and 'List of illustrations'. Translation of *3*.

To date, no English translation has appeared of the definitive 1963 text (*6*).

Nadja has also been translated into Czech, Dutch, German, Greek, Italian, Japanese, Portuguese, Serbo-Croat, Spanish and Swedish.

III. RELATED WORKS BY ANDRÉ BRETON

11. *L'Amour fou*, Gallimard, Coll. Folio, 1976.
12. *Arcane XVII*, Union Générale d'Edition, Coll. 10/18, 1965.
13. *Les Champs magnétiques*, with Philippe Soupault, Gallimard, Coll. Poésie, 1971.
14. *Clair de Terre*, Gallimard, Coll. Poésie, 1966.
15. *Entretiens 1913-1952*, Gallimard, 1952.
16. *Manifestes du surréalisme*, Gallimard, Coll. Idées, 1963.
17. *Les Pas perdus*, Gallimard, Coll. Idées, 1970.
18. *Perspective cavalière*, Gallimard, 1970.
19. *Signe ascendant*, Gallimard, Coll. Poésie, 1968.
20. *Les Vases communicants*, Gallimard, Coll. Idées, 1970.

For fuller information on Breton's writings, see Michael Sheringham, *André Breton: a bibliography*, London: Grant & Cutler, 1972.

IV. CRITICAL MATERIAL SPECIFICALLY ON 'NADJA'

21. Pierre Albouy, 'Signe et signal dans *Nadja*', *Europe*, 483-84 (juill.-août 1969), 234-39.
22. Jean Arrouye, 'La photographie dans *Nadja*', *Mélusine*, IV, Lausanne: L'Age d'Homme, 1982, 123-51.
23. Michel Beaujour, 'Qu'est-ce que *Nadja*?', *La Nouvelle Revue Française*, XV, 172 (avril 1967), 780-99.
24. Marc Bertrand, '*Nadja*: un secret de fabrication surréaliste', *L'Information Littéraire*, XXI, 2 (mars-avril 1979), 82-90 and 3 (mai-juin 1979), 125-30.
25. Peter Bürger, 'Bretons *Nadja* (1928)', in *Der französische Surrealismus. Studien zum Problem der avantgardistischen Literatur*, Frankfurt a.M.: Athenäum Verlag, 1971, 124-38.
26. Roger Cardinal, 'Nadja and Breton', *Univ. of Toronto Quarterly*, XLI, 3 (Spring 1972), 185-99.
27. Robert Champigny, 'The first person in *Nadja*', in *About French Poetry from Dada to 'Tel Quel'*, ed. Mary Ann Caws, Detroit: Wayne State U.P., 1974, 242-53.
28. Jean-Paul Clébert, 'Traces de Nadja', *Revue des Sciences Humaines*, LVI, 184 (oct.-déc. 1981), 79-94.
29. Victor Crastre, *André Breton. Trilogie surréaliste — 'Nadja', 'Les Vases communicants', 'L'Amour fou'*, Société d'Édition d'Enseignement supérieur, 1971.
30. Claude Estève, '*Nadja*', *La Nouvelle Revue Française*, 182 (1 nov. 1928), 736-40.

31. Jean Gaulmier, 'Remarques sur le thème de Paris chez André Breton de *Nadja* à *L'Amour fou*', *Travaux de linguistique et de littérature édités par le Centre de philologie et de littératures romanes de l'Univ. de Strasbourg*, IX, 2 (1971), 159-69.

32. Renée Riese Hubert, 'The coherence of Breton's *Nadja*', *Contemporary Literature*, X, 2 (Spring 1969), 241-52.

33. Louisa Jones, '*Nadja* and the language of poetic fiction', *Dada/Surrealism*, 3 (1973), 45-52.

34. Robert-A. Jouanny, '*Nadja*' — *André Breton*, Hatier, Profil d'une œuvre No. 36, 1972.

35. Sydney Levy, 'André Breton's *Nadja* and automatic writing', *Dada/Surrealism*, 2 (1972), 28-31.

36. Carlos Lynes, 'Surrealism and the novel: Breton's *Nadja*', *French Studies*, XX, 4 (Oct. 1966), 366-87.

37. Marcel Mariën, 'Mort de Nadja', *Les Lèvres Nues*, 12 (fév. 1975), n.p.

38. Claude Martin, '*Nadja* et le mieux-dire', *Revue d'histoire littéraire de France*, LXXII, 2 (mars-avril 1972), 274-86.

39. Georges Mary, 'Les deux convulsions de Nadja ou le livre soufflé', *Mélusine*, III, Lausanne: L'Age d'Homme, 1982, 207-14.

40. J.H. Matthews, 'Désir et merveilleux dans *Nadja* d'André Breton', *Symposium*, XXVII, 3 (Fall 1973), 246-68.

41. Roger Navarri, '*Nadja* ou l'écriture malheureuse', *Europe*, LI, 528 (avril 1973), 186-95.

41a. ——, *André Breton* — '*Nadja*', Presses Universitaires de France, Etudes littéraires, No.11, 1986.

42. Gerald Prince, 'La fonction métanarrative dans *Nadja*', *The French Review*, XLIX, 3 (Feb. 1976), 342-46.

43. Stéphane Sarkany, '*Nadja* ou la lecture du monde objectif', *Mélusine*, IV, Lausanne: L'Age d'Homme, 1982, 101-09.

44. Roger Shattuck, 'The Nadja file', *Cahiers de l'association internationale pour l'étude de Dada et du surréalisme*, 1 (1966), 49-56.

45. Gisela Steinwachs, *Mythologie des Surrealismus oder die Rückverwandlung von Kultur in Natur: eine strukturale Analyse von Bretons 'Nadja'*, Neuwied/Berlin: Luchterhand, 1971.

46. Pierre Testud, '*Nadja*, ou la métamorphose', *Revue des Sciences Humaines*, XXXVI, 144 (oct.-déc. 1971), 579-89.

V. RELATED CRITICAL MATERIAL

47. Sarane Alexandrian, 'André Breton et l'amour surréaliste', in *Les Libérateurs de l'amour*, Seuil, 1977, pp.207-55.

48. Ferdinand Alquié, *Philosophie du surréalisme*, Flammarion, 1955.

49. Anna Balakian, *André Breton. Magus of Surrealism*, New York: Oxford University Press, 1971.

50. Maurice Blanchot, 'Le demain joueur. (Sur l'avenir du surréalisme)', *La Nouvelle Revue Française*, XV, 172 (avr. 1967), 863-88.

51. Marguerite Bonnet, *André Breton. Naissance de l'aventure surréaliste*, Corti, 1975.

52. ——, 'Le surréalisme d'André Breton: un projet d'existence', *L'Information littéraire*, XXIII, 1 (jan.-fév. 1971), 24-29.

53. Jean Bruno, 'André Breton et la magie quotidienne', *Revue métapsychique*, 27 (jan.-fév. 1954), 97-121.

54. Roger Cardinal, 'André Breton: the surrealist sensibility', *Mosaic*, I, 2 (Jan. 1968), 112-26.

55. ——, 'Surrealist beauty', *Forum for Modern Language Studies*, IX, 4 (Oct. 1974), 348-56.

56. ——, 'Soluble city: the surrealist perception of Paris', *Architectural Design*, XLVIII, 2-3 (1978), 143-49.

57. Michel Carrouges, *André Breton et les données fondamentales du surréalisme*, Gallimard, 1950.

58. Julien Gracq, *André Breton: quelques aspects de l'écrivain*, Corti, 1948.

59. Rosalind Krauss, 'The photographic conditions of surrealism', *October*, 19 (Winter 1981), 3-34.

60. Michel Leiris, *L'Age d'homme*, Livre de Poche, 1966.

61. André Pieyre de Mandiargues, *Le Désordre de la mémoire. Entretiens avec Francine Mallet*, Gallimard, 1975.

62. Jules Monnerot, *La Poésie moderne et le sacré*, Gallimard, 1945.

63. Maurice Nadeau, *Histoire du surréalisme*, Seuil, 1945.

64. José Pierre, *Surréalisme et anarchie*, Editions Plasma, 1983.

65. Albert Py, 'De l'amour et du comportement lyrique chez André Breton', in *Hommages à Marcel Raymond*, Corti, 1967, 265-74.

66. Robert S. Short, 'The politics of surrealism, 1920-36', *Journal of Contemporary History*, I, 2 (1966), 3-25.

67. Sara D. Tulczyjew, 'André Breton and "Hasard Objectif"', unpublished M.A. dissertation, University of Calgary, 1980.

CRITICAL GUIDES TO FRENCH TEXTS

edited by

Roger Little, Wolfgang van Emden, David Williams